XGen Essentials:

Long Hair Creation with Splines in Maya

XGen Essentials:

Long Hair Creation with Splines in Maya

Balgum Song

XGen Essentials: Long Hair Creation with Splines in Maya

Copyright © 2024 by Balgum Song

All rights reserved. No part of this publication may be reproduced, distributed, or transmitted in any form or by any means, including photocopying, recording, or other electronic or mechanical means, without the prior written permission of the copyright holder, except for brief quotations contained in critical reviews and certain other non-commercial uses permitted by copyright law.

For permission requests, please contact the author at:
Email: sbu1977@dongseo.ac.kr

This book is intended for educational purposes and provides instructional content on how to use XGen in Maya to create long hair. The information, methods, and techniques described in this book have been tested in multiple versions of Maya, but the author does not guarantee the same results in all software environments. Maya is a trademark of Autodesk, Inc. and this book is not affiliated with or endorsed by Autodesk.

ISBN: [979-8-342-81235-1]
First Edition: 2024

Self-Published by Balgum Song

Acknowledgment

I would like to express my deepest gratitude to Bruno Tornisielo and The Gnomon Workshop for their tutorial, *"Creating a Female Hairstyle for Production with Maya XGen"*. Their teachings were a great help in understanding XGen and were an important reference for the sections in this book. I would also like to thank the Maya Learning Channel and Bob McAfee, as some of their lessons combined with my own experience and insights helped me complete this book. Their YouTube tutorials were a great help in refining the techniques I applied in class.

I would especially like to thank April Lissell and Pailin for allowing me to use images of their beautiful hair as reference material. They were instrumental in inspiring and guiding me in creating the hair featured in this project.

Beyond that, the dedication and motivation of my family has been a huge help, and I hope this book will help many people who want to create realistic hair.

Table of Contents

1. Basics with XGen Hair Creation 1

    1.1 Preparing for XGen 1

    1.2 XGen Types for Creating Hair and Fur 6

    1.3 Exploring XGen Fundamentals with a Simple Sphere 11

    1.4 Primitives 16

    1.5 Preview/Output 23

    1.6 Modifiers 31

    1.7 Utilities 38

    1.8 Expressions 40

2. Creating Long Hair with XGen Splines 44

    2.1 Creating a Scalp Geometry 45

    2.2 Scalp Geometry UV Mapping 46

    2.3 Setting Up Curves for Each Part of the Hair 48

    2.4 Simple Surface Generation 50

    2.5 Duplicating and Mirroring Curves 51

    2.6 Finalizing Curves 52

3. Shaping Hair Layers for Realism 54

    3.1 Creating Top Hair 54

    3.2 Creating Braid Hair 62

    3.3 Creating Side Hair 76

3.4 Creating Low Side Hair 82

3.5 Creating Bangs 88

3.6 Creating a Bun 89

3.7 Creating Long Hair (Left, Right, and Back) 91

3.8 Creating Sideburns (Left and Right) 93

3.9 Creating Messy Hair at the Back 94

3.10 Creating Flyaway Hair 95

4. Enhancing Hair with XGen Modifiers 99

4.1 Modifiers: Top Hair 100

4.2 Modifiers: Braid Hair 104

4.3 Modifiers: Other Hair Descriptions 105

5. Lighting and Shading XGen Hair 109

5.1 Setting Up the Render Camera 109

5.2 Adding Lights 110

5.3 Adding Shaders 113

5.4 Render Settings 120

6. Simulating Hair Movement with XGen 129

6.1 Activating the Hair System from Primitives 130

6.2 Creating an AnimWire Modifier for Dynamic Curves 132

Index 136

Introduction

About the Author

I have been a professor at Dongseo University since 2015, specializing in the technical aspects of Maya, including rigging, nCloth, XGen hair and fur, and Python plugins. In my classes, I teach students how to create realistic fur and hair using XGen, giving them the freedom to design their own fur animations and hairstyles. Students have the opportunity to realize their own unique ideas and turn them into animations with furry animals or custom hairstyles.

Over the years, I've seen my students' interest in creating realistic hair and fur, and I've been motivated to share my knowledge more broadly. This book is the result of references gained from teaching XGen Hair in my classes. It covers everything from the basics to advanced techniques and uses reference images to guide you step-by-step through the process of creating hair. Each chapter is hands-on practical experience and accessible to learners of all levels.

I have tested the techniques described in this book with various versions of Maya, and have tried to make the instructions compatible across all versions. However, due to bugs in the expression editor, I recommend avoiding Maya 2020. If you encounter difficulties or need a Maya reference file to follow along with each chapter, please email me for help.

Best regards,

Balgum Song

Email: sbu1977@dongseo.ac.kr

Book Description/Chapter Overview

"XGen Essentials: Long Hair Creation with Splines in Maya" is a comprehensive guide aimed at helping students, professionals, and hobbyists master the art of creating realistic hair in 3D using XGen in Maya. This book walks readers through practical, step-by-step instructions on using splines for long hair creation. The topics covered range from preparing geometry, working with curves, and applying modifiers to rendering and simulating realistic hair.

To enhance your learning experience, the project Maya file used in the book is available through a link to my Google Drive.

https://drive.google.com/drive/folders/12UWRl4401xakvlovVOvt6MKTsoFWd2ah?usp=sharing

This project was created using Maya 2023. If you are working with an older version of Maya and encounter compatibility issues, please feel free to email me, and I'll do my best to assist you in adjusting the file for your version.

Whether you're a beginner or a seasoned Maya user, this book provides a rich set of tools and techniques that will help you elevate your XGen hair creation skills to the next level.

Here is a brief overview of what is covered in this book:

- **Chapter 1: Basics with XGen Hair Creation**

    Understand the basic tools and settings in XGen, including how to prepare geometry, set up the workspace, and explore key features such as primitives and modifiers.

- **Chapter 2: Creating Long Hair with XGen Splines**

    This chapter focuses on the practical steps for generating long hair using XGen splines. You'll learn how to create scalp geometry, apply UV mapping, and set up curves to guide the hair placement. The chapter covers creating long sections of hair such as the back and overall structure for long hair, laying the foundation for detailed hairstyles explored in later chapters.

- **Chapter 3: Shaping Hair Layers for Realism**

    Explore techniques to create detailed hair layers. This chapter focuses on how to shape, refine, and adjust each hair section for realistic hair volume and flow. This chapter walks you through how to design various hair sections such as braids, sides, and bangs.

- **Chapter 4: Enhancing Hair with XGen Modifiers**

    Learn how to apply clumping, noise, coil, and cut modifiers to enhance the texture and shape of your hair. Learn to manipulate modifiers for dynamic, lifelike results.

- **Chapter 5: Lighting and Shading XGen Hair**

    Set up Arnold lighting and apply shaders to the XGen hair for a realistic render. Get tips on adding color variation, using HDRI maps, and fine-tuning hair reflections.

- **Chapter 6: Simulating Hair Movement with XGen**

    This chapter covers two approaches to simulating hair in Maya: the top-down method (using the hair system in primitives) and the bottom-up method (using dynamic curves with AnimWire Modifiers). Learn how to realistically simulate the movement of hair.

Each chapter is packed with practical examples, visual guides, and instructions to help you confidently work with XGen hair creation in Maya. Whether you're a beginner or an experienced user, this book will provide you with valuable insights and techniques to take your XGen skills to the next level.

XGen Essentials: Long Hair Creation with Splines in Maya

1. Basics with XGen Hair Creation

XGen is a powerful tool for creating scenes filled with complex objects like realistic hair, fur, grass, marbles, and pebbles. This guide will walk beginners through the process of efficiently creating long hair using XGen, from understanding the tools to setting up workspace properly. Before diving into creating character hair, it's important to understand XGen's menus, tools, and how to set up your project for optimal performance. This chapter covers the basics of XGen, and those who want to begin practical hair creation can start with Chapter 2: Creating Long Hair with XGen Splines

1.1 Preparing for XGen

Ensuring XGen Toolkit is Active

Before you start working in XGen, make sure that the XGen Toolkit is correctly loaded in Maya. Follow these steps:
- Go to **Windows > Settings/Preferences > Plug-in Manager**.
- Ensure that **xgenToolkit.mll** is enabled.

This step is important to acess all the XGen features you need.

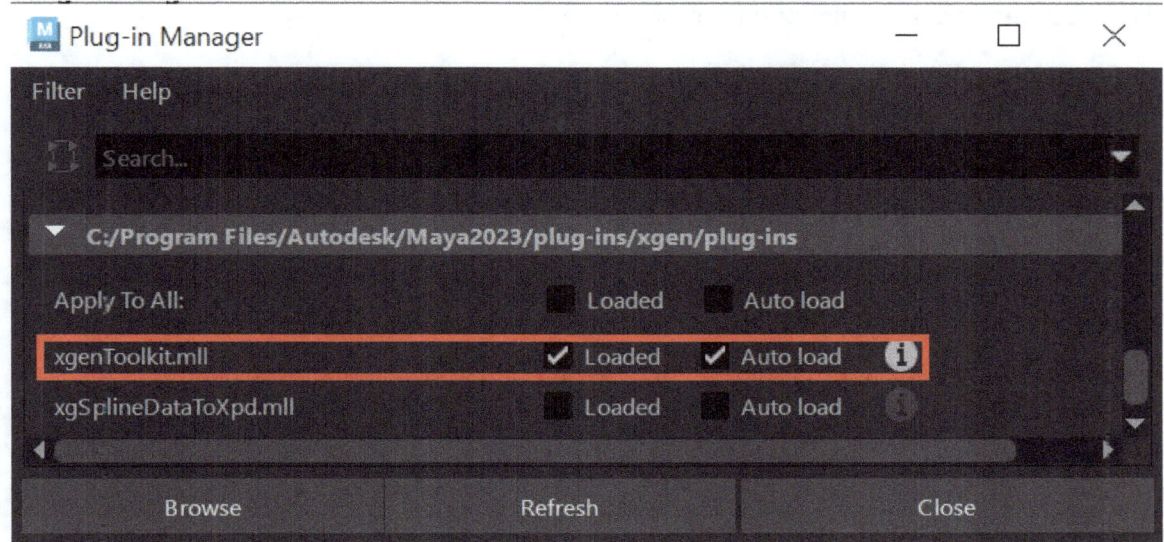

Figure 1.1.1 xgenToolkit.mll

Before Applying XGen

Before applying XGen to your geometry, follow these best practices to avoid potential issues:

Freeze Transformations and Delete History: Always **Freeze Transformations** and **Delete History** on your geometry before applying XGen. Otherwise you may encounter various issues, such as incorrect deformations and inaccurate Ptex resolution.

Model in Real-World Scale: Make sure that your character is modeled in real-world scale. This is essential for achieving realistic animation and simulation, especially when working with light sources.

Project File Setup: XGen can be resource-intensive, especially when dealing with complex hair and fur simulations. For better performance and data management, set up a project file. This will allow to store all XGen-related data, including maps and settings, in an organized manner. To do this:

- If you don't have a project file yet, go to **File > Project Window** and create one with the desired location and name.

- If you already have a project file, make sure to set it by going to **File > Set Project**.

Setting up the correct project file is essential for loading XGen data correctly. If you get it wrong, you may end up with missing hairs and fur or improper loading.

Avoid Triangular Faces: Always aim to keep geometry with square (quad) faces. Triangular faces can cause undesirable results when bending and deforming the hair.

Ensure Proper UV Unwrapping: UVs should be unwrapped correctly and set within the 0-1 UV space to avoid texture and map distortion.

Neutral Pose and Symmetry: Position your character in a neutral, symmetrical pose, with the head pointing along the Z-axis. Incorrect orientation can cause problems fur mirroring.

Use Scalp Geometry: Instead of applying XGen directly to the character's geometry, it's recommended to create separate scalp geometry. This improves performance and control when styling the hair.

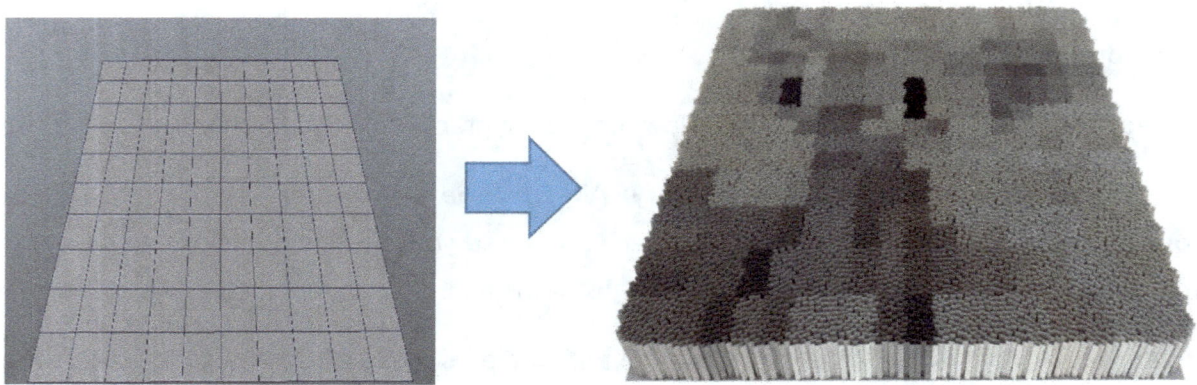

Figure 1.1.2 Subdivision Width & Height: 10, Scale: 10

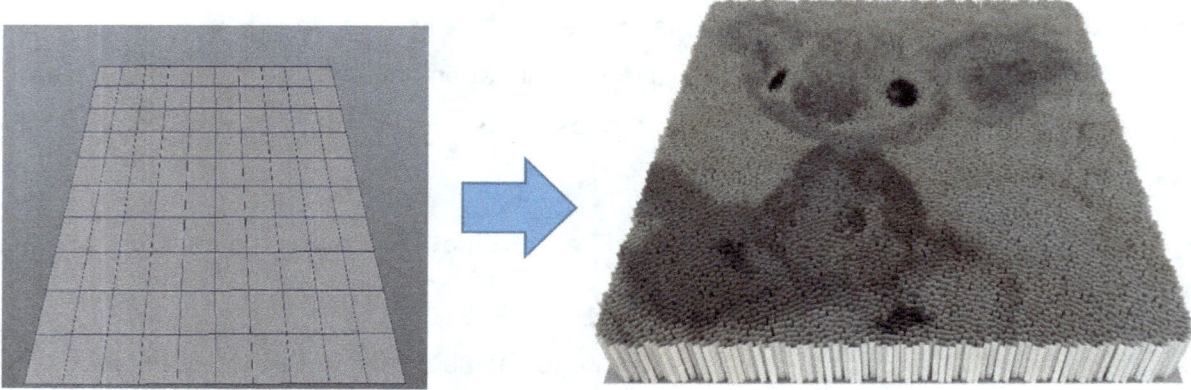

Figure 1.1.3 Subdivision Width & Height: 10, Scale: 1

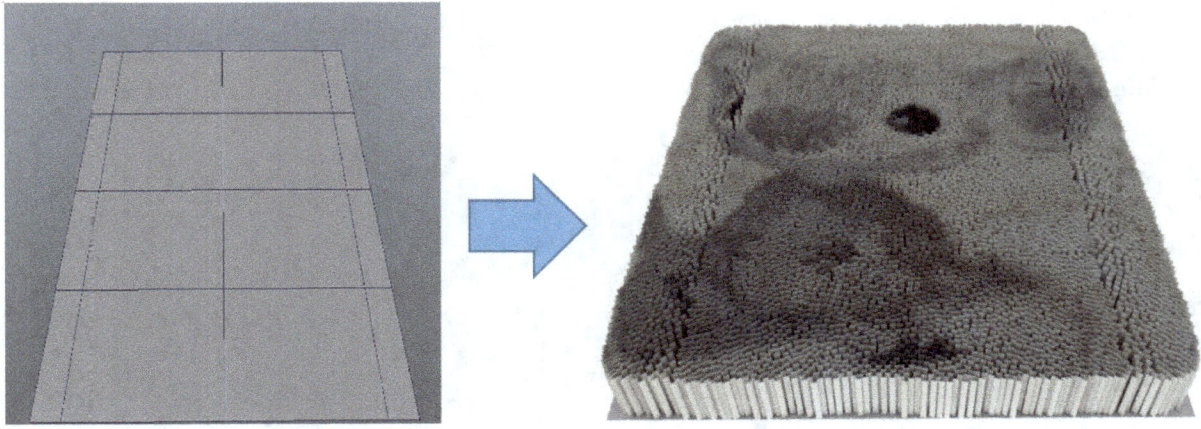

Figure 1.1.4 Subdivision Width & Height: 4, Scale: 1, Change Face Size With No UV Correction

Figure 1.1.5 Subdivision Width & Height: 1, Scale: 10

Adjusting the subdivision levels and scale helps control the density and behavior of the hair strands. Be careful about changing the face size and not to interfere with UV mapping..

XGen File Structure

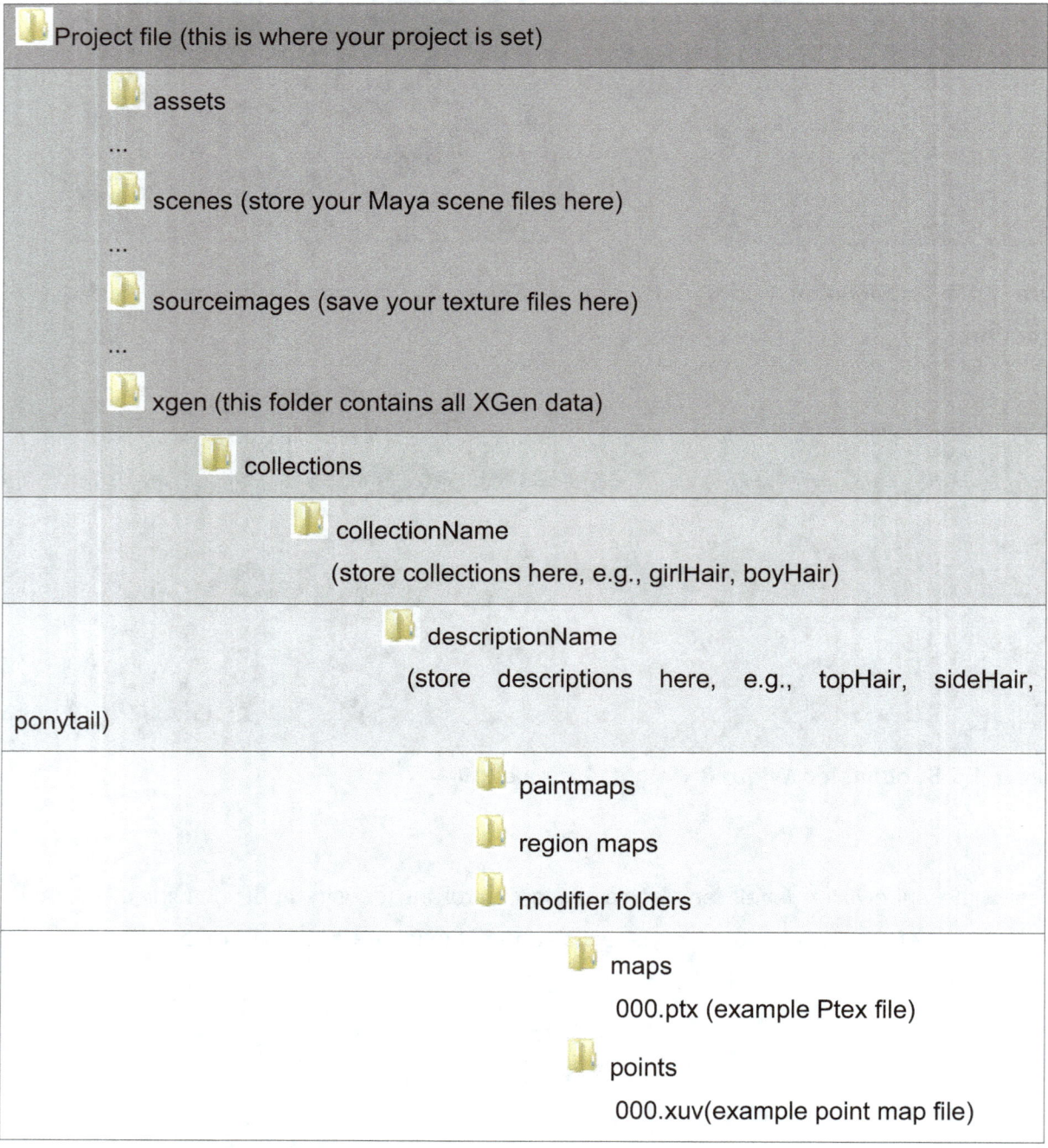

Following this file structure ensures that all XGen-related files, such as paint maps, region maps, and modifier settings, are stored logically and can be accessed without confusion.

Separate layers for complex hair style

When working with complex hairstyles, it's a recommended practice to split the hair into different layers or descriptions within XGen. For example, separate the top, sides, and ponytail into different layers.. This allows you to better manage each section, giving you more control over styling, density, and simulation settings.

By following these best practices, you'll be well-prepared to dive into creating attractive and realistic long hair with XGen.

1.2 XGen Types for Creating Hair and Fur

There are three ways to generate hair and fur in XGen: **Groomable Splines**, **Interactive Grooming Splines (IGS)**, and **Splines**. Each method offers unique advantages and is suitable for generating different types of hair and fur. However, this book focuses specifically on creating long hair using XGen Splines. Throughout each chapter, we will explore this technique in detail and walk you through every step to help you learn how to create realistic long hair with XGen splines. While there are other methods and tools for creating hair and fur, such as nHair, paint effects, and custom Maya fur, this book focuses exclusively on the XGen spline technique.

Groomable Splines: Shaping Hair without Guides
Groomable Splines is a method primarily used for short hair, fur, grass, and similar elements. This method does not use guides, but instead uses a grooming brush to directly shape the hair or fur.

Groomable Splines(use for short hair, fur, grass, etc)	
Summary	Groomable splines use the grooming tools on the Grooming tab to create the shape of hair or fur without guides. When you select a groomable spline, the hair or fur is automatically created, and you can start styling it with a grooming brush to create the desired shape.

Pros	▪ Easy to use and great for styling short hair and fur. ▪ Automatically creates hair or fur at the start, simplifying the initial setup.
Cons	▪ Difficult to use on longer hair and fur as there are no guides for precise control. ▪ Groomable splines are not interactive with primitives, making it difficult to predict the final appearance. ▪ Changing the density after grooming resets the grooming operation and these changes cannot be undone. ▪ Curves are difficult to simulate without guides.

Steps:

1) **Create New Description**

   Select your character, and from the menu sets, choose *Modeling*. From the main menu, go to **Generate > Create Description**, and it creates a pop-up **Create XGen Description** window. Set to **Groomable Splines** (ideal for short hair, fur, grass, etc.). Note that once you choose *Groomable Splines*, you cannot switch to other methods for this description.

Figure 1.2.1 Creating New Description for XGen

2) **Key Settings from the Grooming tab**
   - **Visibility**: Controls the visibility of the groomable splines.
   - **Density**: Adjust the fur density. If you uncheck **Sync**, it will disconnect from the primitives tab density. Note that changing the density after combing will reset the operation.
   - **Sampling**: Choose between **linear**, **nearest**, or **interpolate** settings. These affect how hair interacts with neighboring strands.

- **Mask**: Adjust the mask if grooming is slowing down..
- **Tip/Base Color**: Control the color of the tips and roots of the hair.
- **Display**: Choose between lines or cards. Cards are often preferred because it's easier to visualize hair direction
- **Length and Width**: Set the size of the groomable splines. You can also adjust the width when using cards.
- **TPU (Textures per Unit):** Increase to improve resolution (recommended to set to 15 when exporting groom data).

3) **Brush Tools**
- **Length/Width**: Incrementally adjust the length and width, or set a final target length/width. Set **Increment** to a negative values and **Goal Length/Width** to 0 will able to reduce the size..
- **Pose**: A combination of orientation and bend adjustments.
- **Orient/Bend**: Orient controls the direction of the brush stroke, and bend affects the top of the hair.
- **Elevation**: Adjusts areas to bend towards or away from the surface, but avoid exceeding **Goal Angle** 30° for best results.
- **Noise**: Add noise to the spline.
- **Attract/Repel:** Pinch or push hair to create clumps or disperse strands.
- **Part Brush**: Slightly harder than repel and creates harder lines
- **Twist**: Rotates around from the center of the spline.
- **Smooth**: Blends the splines within the brush, averaging their shape with all splines in the radius.
- **Region**: Assign a color to the area by the brush.
- **Mask:** Allows to paint a mask onto the spline area.
- **Eraser**: Removes Length, Orientation, and Bend strokes.

Interactive Grooming Splines (IGS): Intuitive Guide and Primitive Styling
Interactive Grooming Splines (IGS) provide a more intuitive way to style hair and fur. This method includes guides and modifiers, and its own set of grooming brushes so you can interact directly with individual hairs.

Interactive Grooming Splines (IGS)	
Summary	IGS introduces a new method for styling hair and fur, providing a more intuitive experience. Groom guides and individual hairs directly without the need for complex modifier stacks or additional XGen folders..
Pros	▪ Intuitive grooming, allowing you to adjust individual hair strands for finer details. ▪ No need for extra folders or modifier stacks, simplifying workflow. ▪ Sculpt layers allow for blending techniques similar to those in Photoshop. ▪ No limitations on painting texture maps, unlike traditional XGen, which relies on Ptex maps.
Cons	▪ Limited support for expressions, which can be less efficient when creating complex fur or hair. ▪ Difficult to work with long hair as guide curve points cannot be easily selected. ▪ Lack of mirroring capabilities, but this limitation may be addressed in a future update.

Steps:

1) **Create Interactive Groom Splines**

   Start by selecting geometry. From the main menu choose **Generate> Create Interactive Groom Splines** to generate interactive groom splines.

2) **Modify Guides and Primitives**

   Select the new description from the from the **XGen Interactive Groom Editor** and press **Add modifiers** to apply such as clump, noise, or displacement to adjust the hair. You can also add sculpt layers to blend different grooming effects.

XGen Essentials: Long Hair Creation with Splines in Maya

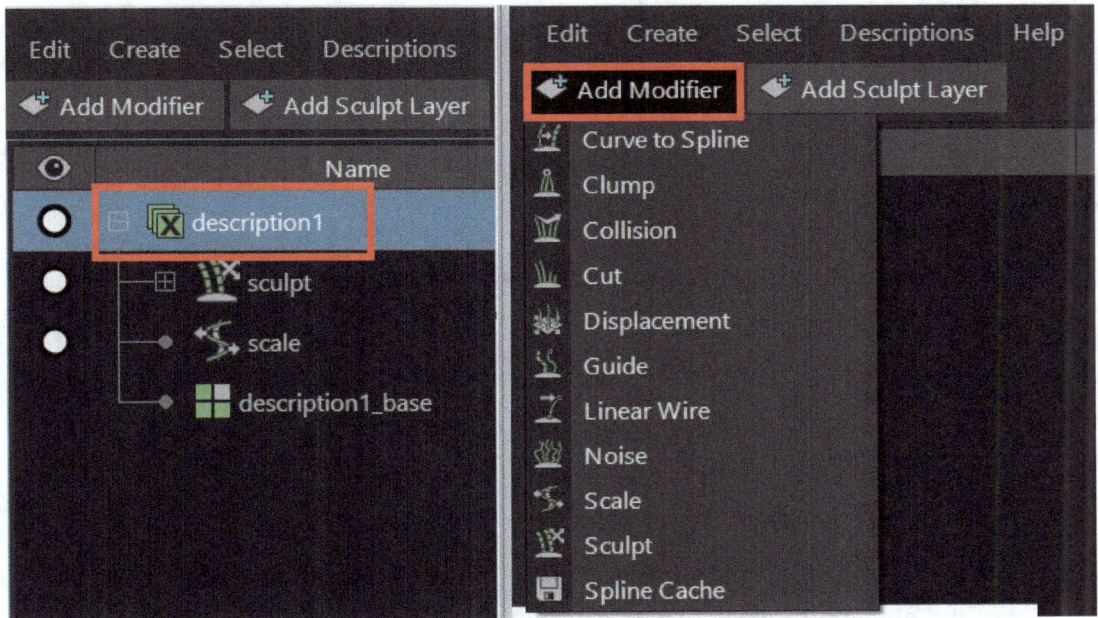

Figure 1.2.2 Add Modifiers for Interactive Groom Splines

3) **Brush Tools**

   From **Generate>Interative Grooming Tools**, use brushes like comb, part, grab, and freeze to style the hair.

Splines: Detailed Control for Long Hair and Complex Styles

Splines are a powerful way to create realistic hair, especially long hair. This approach is used to interpolate primitives using shaping guides. Expressions give you more control over splines, making them ideal for creating natural-looking hair.

Splines(use for long hair, vines, etc)	
Summary	The Splines method uses guides to style hair. Once the guides are shaped, the primitives are automatically interpolated based on the guide shapes. This method is excellent for creating long hair and can be further enhanced by using expressions that simulate more complex hair movements.

Pros	▪ Detailed and precise control over hair shape with guides. ▪ Supports expressions for advanced hair creation (e.g., adding stray hairs or controlling curliness). ▪ Works well for both short and long hair.
Cons	▪ Time-consuming to shape each guide individually. ▪ Sensitive to path directories, meaning that once descriptions and collection names are set, it can be difficult to change it later.. ▪ Limited control over the final detail of individual hair strands. ▪ Only supports Ptex maps, which can be limiting when painting other types of texture maps. ▪ Clump modifiers need to be placed at the beginning of the modifier stack for proper effect, and clump modifiers should be placed first in the stack in order.

In chapter two, you'll learn more about how to implement each method for different hair types and styles, starting with setting up hair per layer.

1.3 Exploring XGen Fundamentals with a Simple Sphere

1) **Create a sphere**
- Go to **Create > Polygon Primitives > Sphere**.
- Resize the sphere to about 8 units. This will serve as the base geometry for generating hair.

2) **Prepare the Sphere for XGen**
- Select the sphere and navigate to **Modify > Freeze Transformations**. This will clean up the scale, rotation, and position so that the XGen process is organized.
- Then, go to **Edit > Delete by Type > History**. This removes any construction history, which can interfere with XGen and cause unexpected issues.
- Go to **File>Set Project** to set the directory for your file, and then save the Maya file with

the sphere.

3) **Start Creating XGen Hair and Fur**

- With the sphere selected, go to **Generate > Create Description**. This opens the XGen Description Editor, where you'll set up the hair for your sphere. Set your description as shown in Figure 1.3.1, and press **Create** to start generating hair.

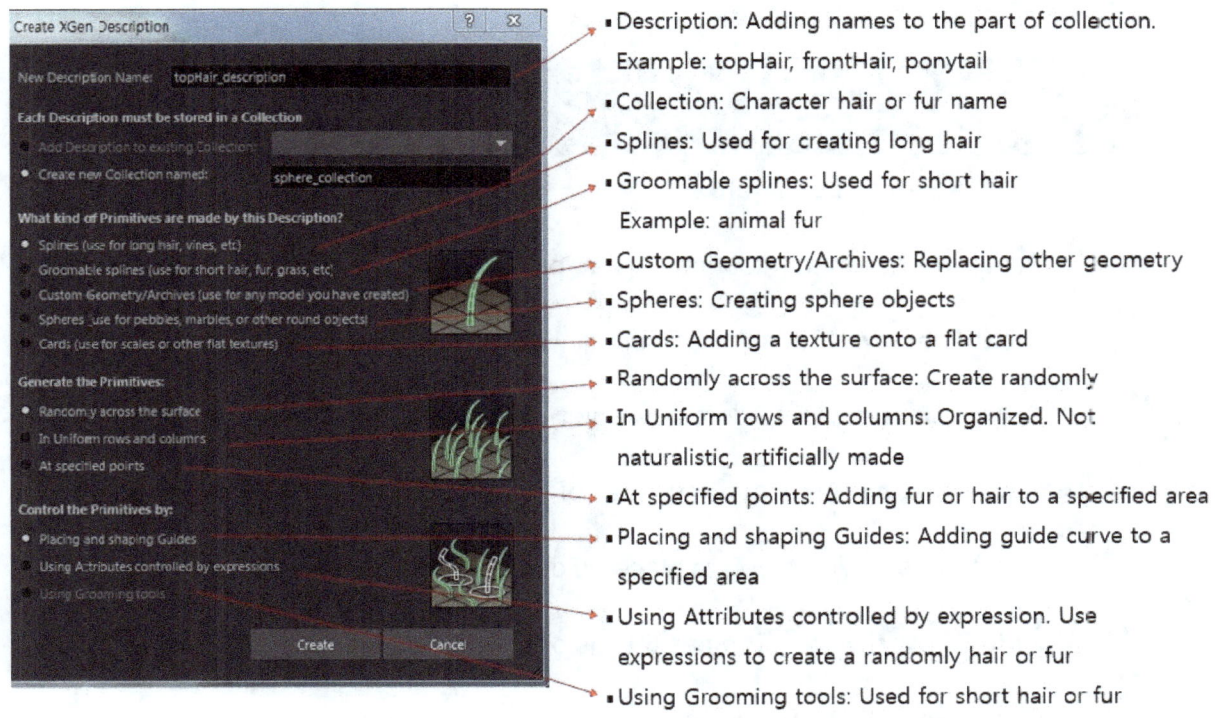

- Description: Adding names to the part of collection. Example: topHair, frontHair, ponytail
- Collection: Character hair or fur name
- Splines: Used for creating long hair
- Groomable splines: Used for short hair Example: animal fur
- Custom Geometry/Archives: Replacing other geometry
- Spheres: Creating sphere objects
- Cards: Adding a texture onto a flat card
- Randomly across the surface: Create randomly
- In Uniform rows and columns: Organized. Not naturalistic, artificially made
- At specified points: Adding fur or hair to a specified area
- Placing and shaping Guides: Adding guide curve to a specified area
- Using Attributes controlled by expression. Use expressions to create a randomly hair or fur
- Using Grooming tools: Used for short hair or fur

Figure 1.3.1 XGen Description Window

4) **Configure the XGen Description**
- Collection Name: This will be the container for all your XGen elements. For example, name it "SphereHairCollection".
- Description Name: The description acts as a layer within the collection. Name it something like "LongHairLayer" to show that you're working with long hair.
- Choose Splines: To create long hair, select the Splines option. This method allows you to place and shape guides across the surface of the sphere, which will ultimately determine the shape and flow of the hair.

Once the description is created, you will notice that hair does not appear yet. This is because the hair will only appear after the guides are added and the XGen preview is generated.

5) **XGen Editor Toolbar Overview**

The XGen Editor provides several useful tools for managing guides and primitives. Here's a quick breakdown of the toolbar options:

Figure 1.3.2 XGen Editor ToolBar

① **Preview**: Shows the geometry's hair primitives.

② **Clear Preview**: Hides the hair primitives.

③ **Create Description**: Add a new layer or description to the collection

④ **Bind Patches**: Adds specific faces of the geometry to the description.

⑤ **Add Guides**: Allows you to place guides on the surface of the geometry.

⑥ **Hide/Show Guides**: Toggles the visibility of guides.

⑦ **Guide Selection**: Allows you to select or lock guides.

⑧ **Mirror Guides**: Mirror guides on one axis to enable symmetrical hair styling.

⑨ **XGen Patch/Geometry**: Toggles between geometry and guides

⑩ **Primitive Selection**: Enable or disable primitive selection.

⑪ **Cull Selected Primitives**: Allows you to select specific parts of the primitive

6) **Add Guide Curves**

Add guide curves to the geometry. Guide curves are not those final rendered curves.

Primitives are those that are going to display in the final renderer, which are automatically generated around the guide curves area.

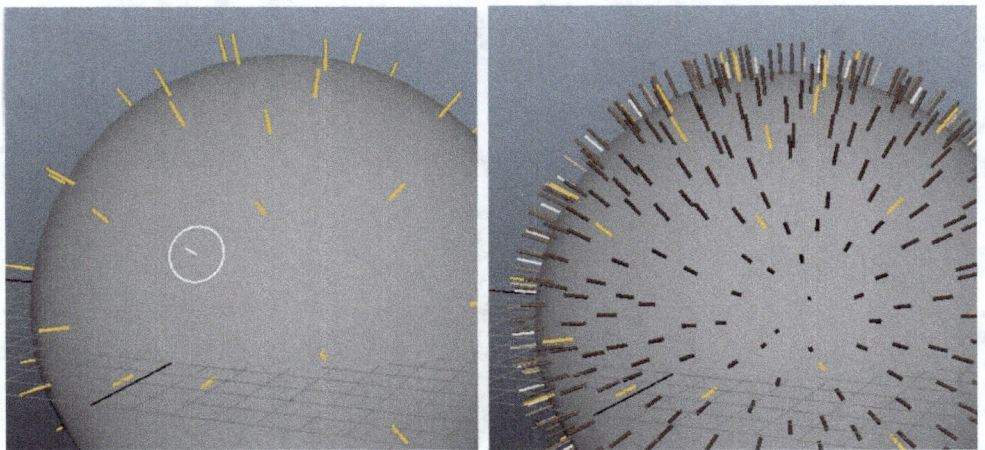

Figure 1.3.3 Guide Curves(Orange) left and Primitives(Brown) right

7) **Adjusting the Shape of Guide Curves**
- To adjust the shape of a guide curve, hover your cursor over the guide, right-click (RMB), and select **Guide Control Points**. This allows you to modify the control points to shape the curve as desired.

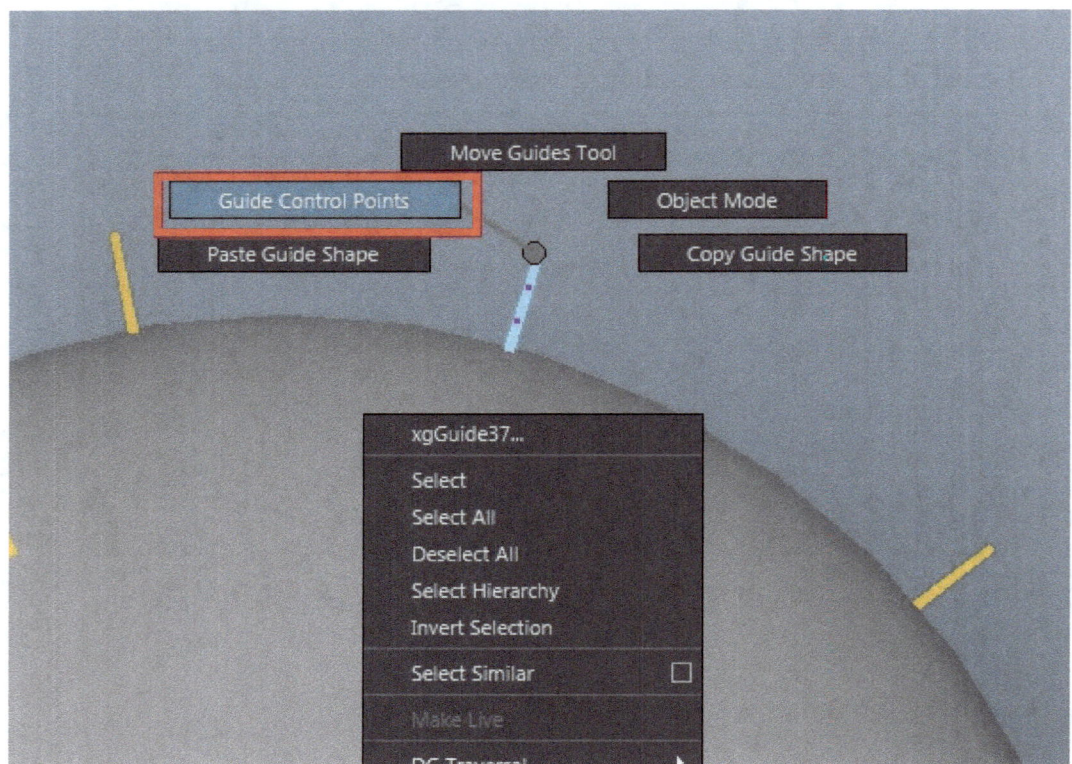

Figure 1.3.4 Adjusting the guide curve shapes

- **Tip**: Alternatively, you can use the **Sculpt Guides** tool from the XGen Menu to manipulate the guide curves more intuitively.

If you need to move an entire guide curve to a new location on your geometry, choose **Add Guides**, hold down the "Ctrl" key, and use the left mouse button (LMB) to reposition the guide curve.

8) **Copy and Paste Guide Shapes**

After adjusting a guide curve to your liking, you can copy its shape and apply it to other guides. To do this:
- Select the guide curve you want to copy, right-click (RMB), and choose **Copy Guide Shape**.
- Next, select another guide curve, right-click (RMB), and choose **Paste Guide Shape**.

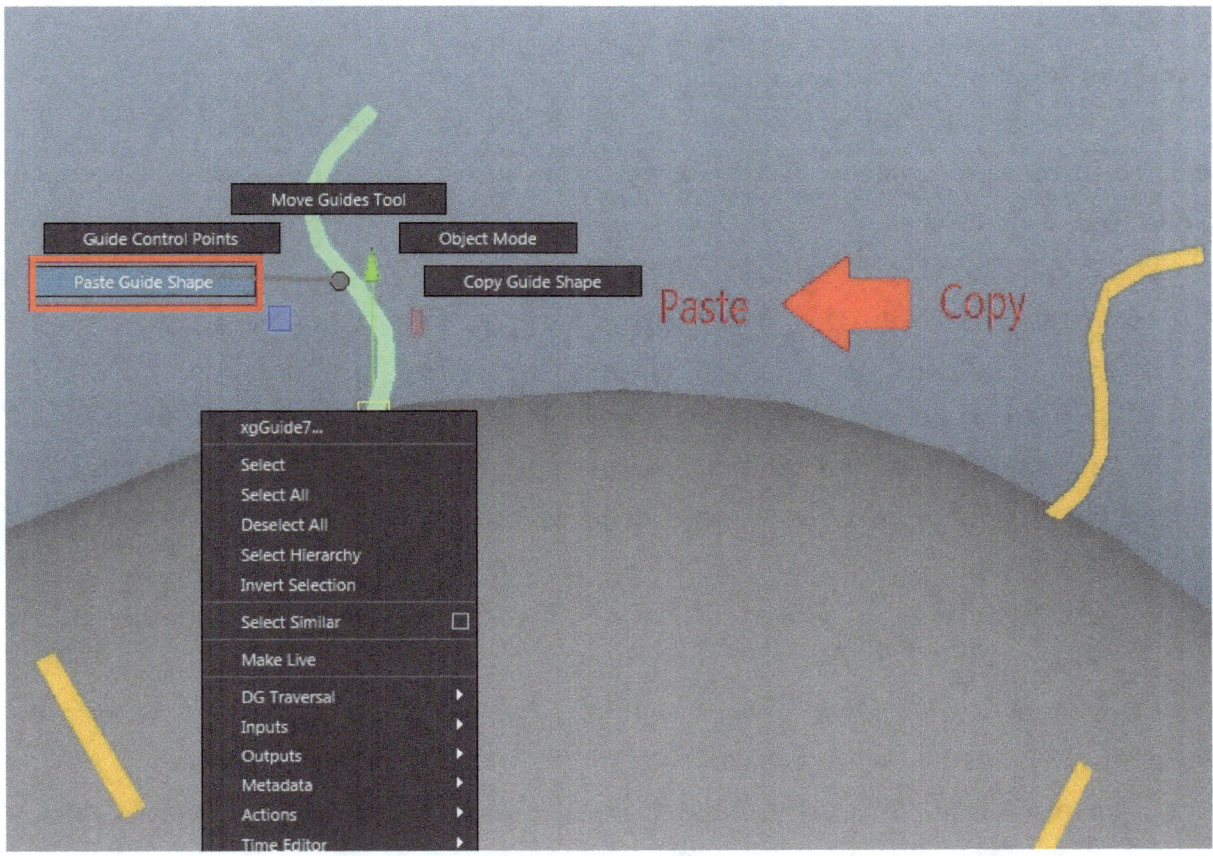

Figure 1.3.5 Copy and Paste Guide Shapes

This is especially useful if you want to maintain consistency across multiple guides or replicate a specific hairstyle pattern..

With these steps, you have successfully set up a basic XGen hair system using spheres. You can continue to refine your guides and primitives to achieve the look you want using the tools and techniques provided.

1.4 Primitives

Primitives are the actual elements that will be rendered in your final scene. They represent the hair or fur and are generated based on the guides you create. In this section, we will explore how to control and manipulate primitives in XGen to achieve the desired look for your hair or fur.

Generator Attributes

The Generator Attributes panel is where you define how your primitives are generated and distributed across the geometry. These settings allow you to control the number, placement, and density of the primitives.

- **Generate Primitives**: Determines how you want to distribute the primitives across the surface of your geometry. You can choose from the following options:
    - **Randomly across the surface**: Distributes primitives randomly across the surface.
    - **In uniform rows and columns**: Places primitives evenly across the geometry.
    - **At specified locations**: Limits the distribution of primitives to specific areas you define.
    - **From XPD File**: Imports a predefined distribution of primitives from an external XPD file.
- **Generator Seed**: Sets a random seed for the placement of primitives. Changing the seed will alter the distribution while maintaining the same number of primitives.
- **Density**: Adjusts the number of primitives on your geometry. Increasing the density adds more hair or fur, while decreasing it removes them.
- **Mask**: Allows you to define specific areas where you want primitives to appear or avoid. This can be controlled by painting a mask onto your geometry.

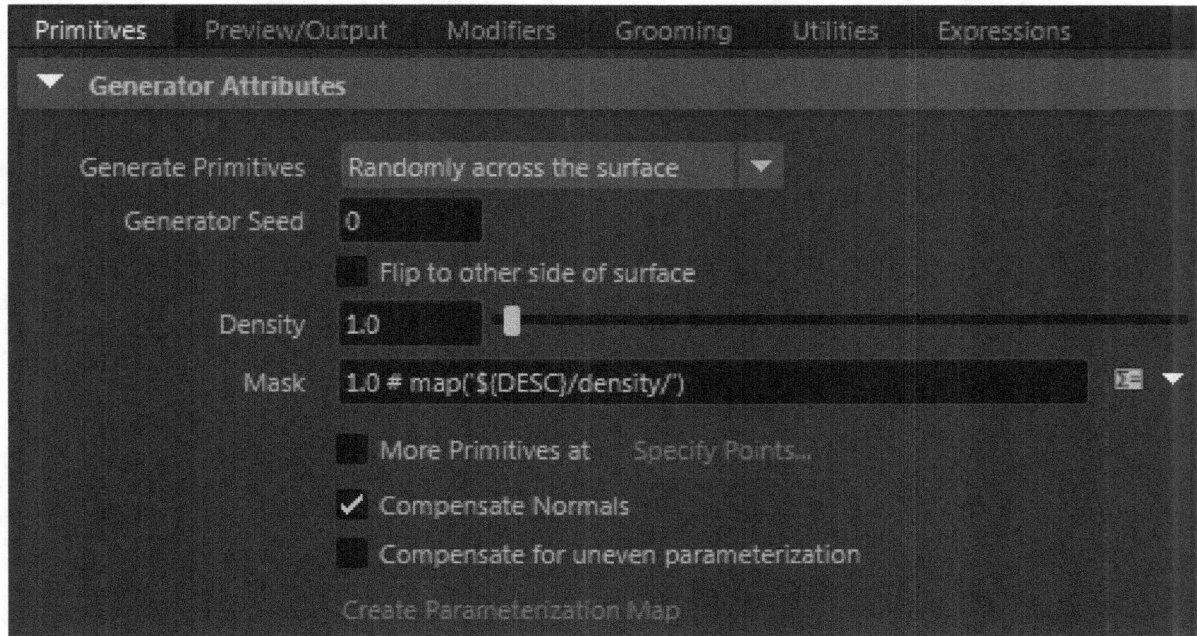

Figure 1.4.1 Generator Attributes

Steps for Creating and Using a Mask

1) Go to **File > Save Scene As** and save the scene before applying the mask. The paint tool will not operate correctly if the file is not saved first.

2) **Create Map**: On the right side of the Mask section, click the arrow ▽ and choose **Create Map**. Set a name for your map, define the resolution to 5 or higher depending on the desired accuracy, and choose a start color (usually start from black).

3) **Create**: Click **Create** to generate the map.

4) **Open 3D Paint Tool**: This tool allows you to paint directly on the geometry. Use black to remove primitives from certain areas and white to add them.

5) **Paint**: Paint the areas where you want to control the presence of primitives.

6) **Save**: Click the save button on the right, next to the Mask attribute, to save the painted mask. Always save your work frequently. When saving, a Ptex file will be created in

your project directory.

7) **More Primitives At**: Under **Generator Attributes** check **More Primitives at** to add more primitives in specific areas by adjusting this option.

8) **Compensate Normals**: This option is enabled by default. It ensures that primitives are evenly distributed even if the face regions of your geometry have uneven sizes.

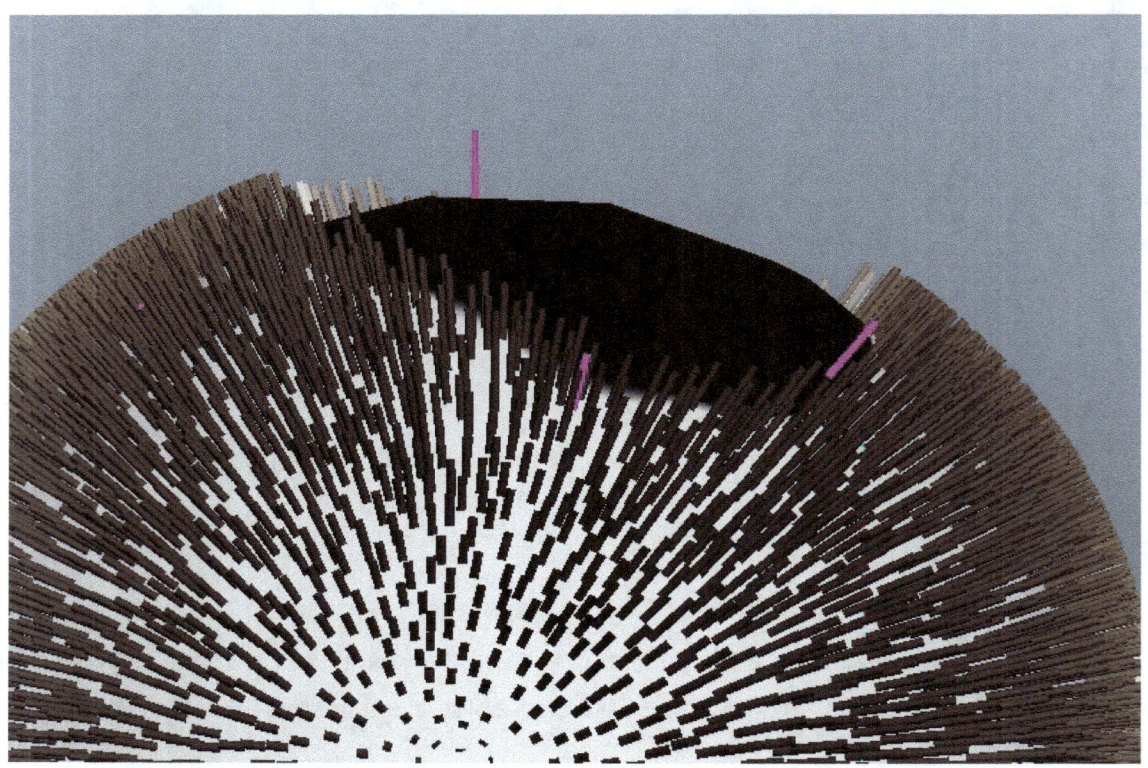

Figure 1.4.2 Applying Mask

9) **Compensate for Uneven Parameterization**: This feature ensures that primitives are placed uniformly, compensating for any variations in face sizes on the geometry. This is essential for creating a smooth, consistent look, particularly on complex surfaces.

Primitive Attributes

Once your primitives are generated, the **Primitive Attributes** panel provides fine control over their appearance and behavior. Here are the key attributes you can adjust

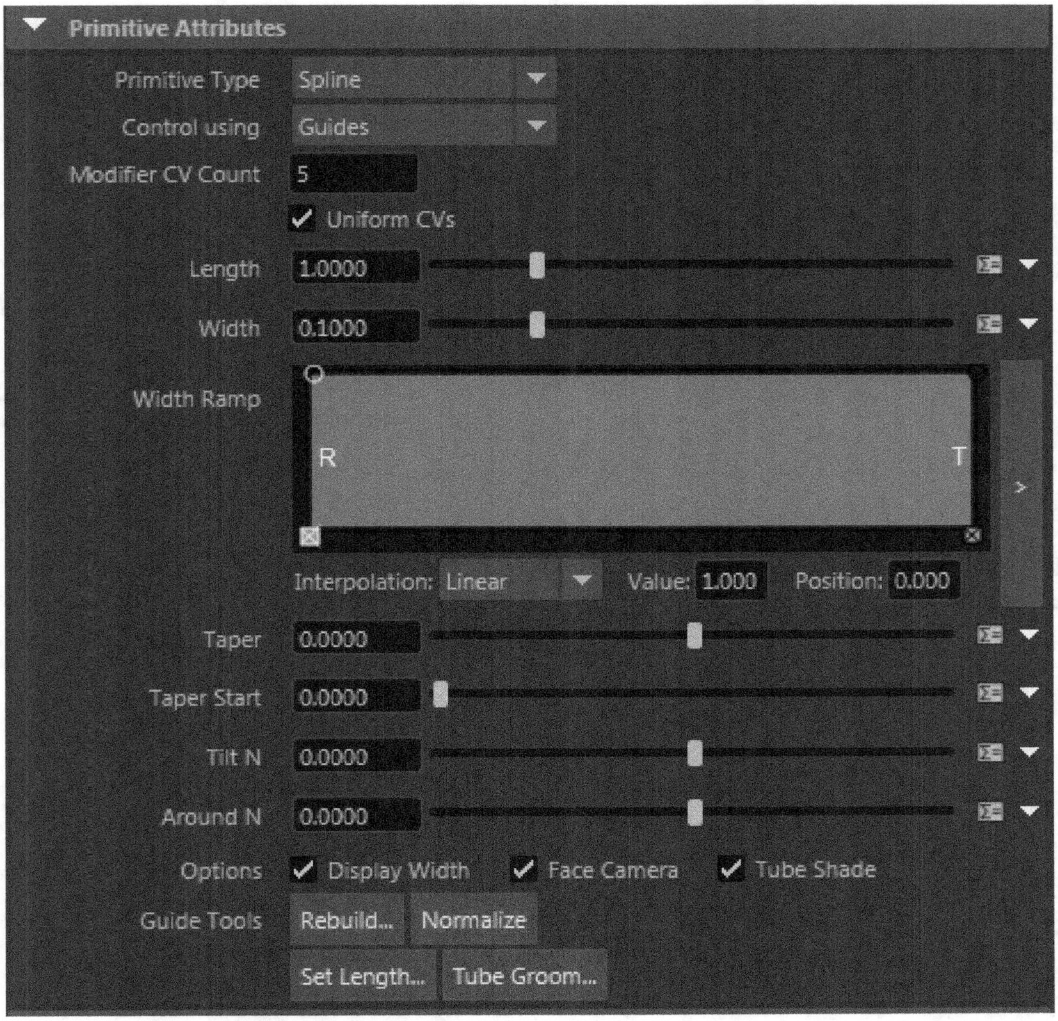

Figure 1.4.3 Primitive Attributes

- **Primitive Type**: Choose the type of primitive you want to use. Options include:
  - ✓ **Archive**: Use pre-created assets as primitives.
  - ✓ **Card**: Generates flat cards for hair, often used for real-time engines.
  - ✓ **Sphere**: Creates spherical primitives.
  - ✓ **Spline**: The default for hair and fur, representing strands of hair.
- **Control using**: Determines whether your primitives are controlled by Attributes or by Guides. This choice affects how you interact with and manipulate the hair.
- **Modifier CV Count**: Sets the number of CVs (Control Vertices) on each primitive. Higher CV counts result in more flexible and detailed hair strands but can increase

computational demands.
- **Length**: Defines the length of the primitives. You can adjust this attribute to scale the hair or fur to your desired length.
- **Width**: Controls the width of the primitives. For hair, this typically starts wider at the root and narrows toward the tip.
- **Width Ramp**: Allows you to adjust the width of the primitives along their length, from the root to the tip. You can create a custom ramp to control the tapering effect.
- **Taper**: Controls how sharply the hair tapers off toward the tip. Increasing the taper value makes the hair appear pointier at the ends.
- **Taper Start**: Specifies where along the length of the primitive the tapering effect should begin.
- **Tilt N**: Adjusts the angle at which the primitive tilts relative to the surface of the geometry. A value of 90 degrees makes the primitive parallel to the face.
- **Around N**: Rotates the primitive around its axis, allowing for additional styling variations.
- **Options**: These options allow you to visualize and control how primitives appear in the viewport.
- **Guide Tools**:
  The following tools are available to help manage and modify the guides that control your primitives:
  - **Rebuild**: Rebuilds the CV count of the selected guides, allowing you to increase or decrease the resolution of your guide curves.
  - **Normalize**: Evenly spaces out the CVs on the guide curves, resulting in smoother curves.
  - **Set Length**: Adjusts the length of the guide curves.
  - **Tube Groom**: Creates guide curves based on the shape of geometry, which can be useful for specific hairstyles or fur patterns.

Region Control

Region Control allows you to further refine how your primitives behave across different areas of your geometry by using Region Masks and Region Maps.

Figure 1.4.4 Region Control

- **Region Mask**: This feature allows you to set an influence range from 0 (no influence) to 1 (full influence). You can create and paint maps to control the distribution and influence of primitives in specific regions of your geometry.
- Region Map: Region maps let you divide your geometry into different colored regions, each with distinct primitive attributes.

Steps for Creating a Region Map:

1) **Create Map**: In the Region Map section, click ▽ **Create Map**. Name your map, set the resolution, and choose a base color.

2) **Add Colors**: Paint different colors onto the map to define separate regions on your geometry.

3) **Save**: **Save** your work to ensure the map is properly stored in your project directory.

By using region control, you can blend or vary the influence of different effects, allowing for more nuanced and complex hairstyles or fur patterns.

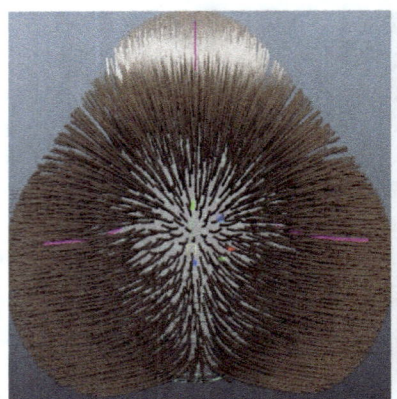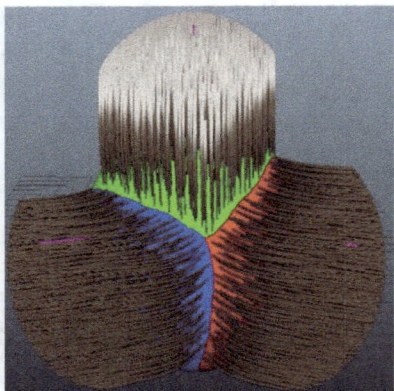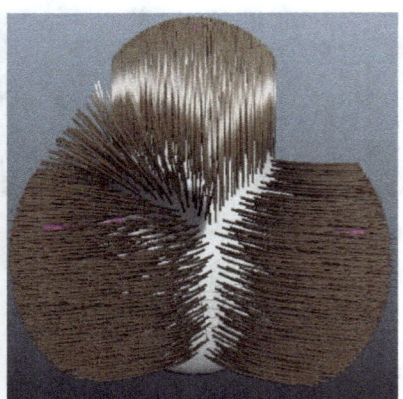

Figure 1.4.5 No Region Map(left), Region Map(middle) and blending Region Mask(right)

With these tools and settings, you now have a strong understanding of how to manage and manipulate primitives in XGen. The flexibility of these attributes and controls gives you the power to create everything from simple fur to complex, stylized hair, all while maintaining control over the final rendered appearance.

1.5 Preview/Output

In XGen, the Preview Settings and Output Settings under the **Preview/Output** tab control how your hair and fur are displayed in the viewport and rendered in the final output. While the preview settings allow you to visualize the primitives during the creation process, the output settings ensure that the final render has the desired textures and shaders applied. This section explains how to set up both preview and output settings for your XGen hair and fur.

Preview Settings

The Preview Settings allow you to control how the primitives appear in the viewport. It's important to note that the preview may not exactly match the final rendered image, but it helps visualize your work in real-time.

Steps to Add Textures to Preview Settings

1) **Access Preview Settings**

    Go to the **Preview Settings** section under the **Preview/Output**.

XGen Essentials: Long Hair Creation with Splines in Maya

2) **Create a Map**

   Click on ▽ **Create Map** under **Preview Settings>Primitive Color**.

   Set the **Map Name, Map Resolution, Start Color** to **White** then press **Create**. You can paint using **3D Paint Tool** or add textures. To add a custom texture, replace the 3D paint texture with your own file texture. This allows you to preview the appearance of your primitives with the actual texture applied, helping you gauge how the final output might look. I will guide you through how to add textures so that **Preview Settings** match the **Output Settings**(final render view) in the next page's Output Settings lesson.

3) **Save the Map**

   After configuring your map, hit 💾 **Save** to store the settings.

4) **Replace the 3D Paint Texture**

   To add a custom texture, replace the 3D paint texture with your own file texture. This allows you to preview the appearance of your primitives with the actual texture applied, helping you gauge how the final output might look.

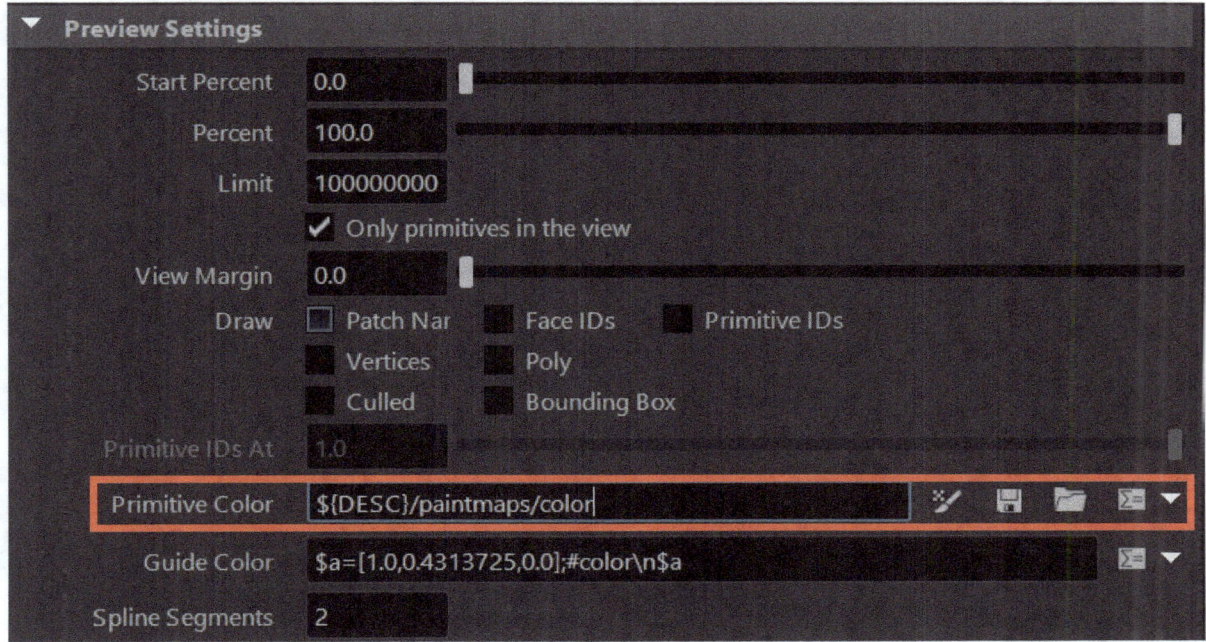

Figure 1.5.1 Preview Settings

By using preview textures, you can make quick adjustments to the look and feel of your hair and fur while working in the viewport.

Output Settings

The Output Settings are crucial for ensuring that your hair and fur look correct in the final rendered image. Applying textures and shaders in the Output Settings involves a more detailed process compared to the Preview Settings. This process ensures that textures are properly applied and visible in the final render.

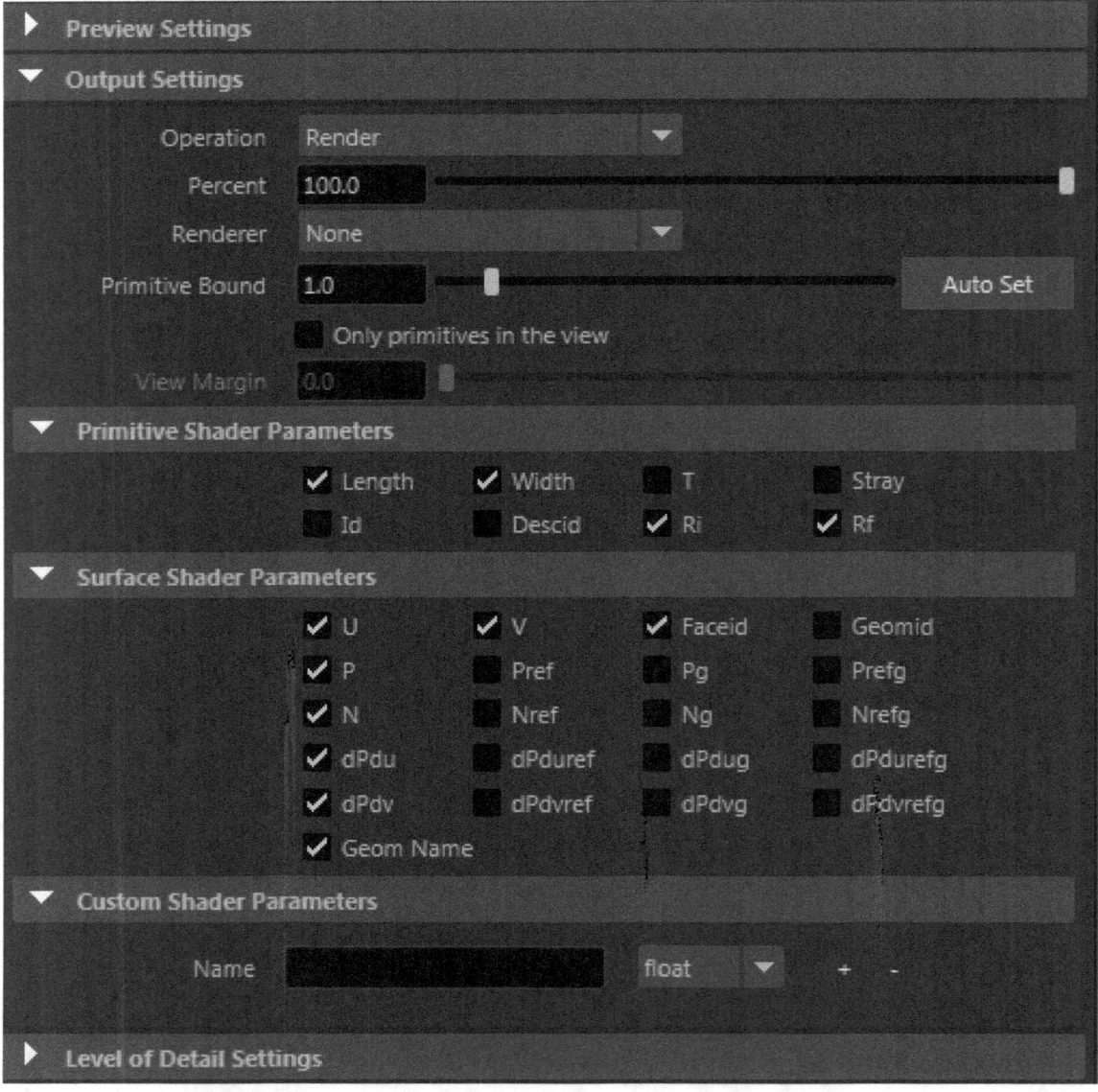

Figure 1.5.2 Output Settings

XGen Essentials: Long Hair Creation with Splines in Maya

Steps to Add Textures to Output Settings

1) **Custom Shader Parameters**

   In the Output Settings, **Custom Shader Parameters** section set a name for the parameter, for example, "finalColor".

   Change the data type from float to color, then click the +plus sign to create the new attribute.

2) **Create a New Attribute**

   Once the new attribute is created (e.g., color finalColor), it will appear under the **Custom Shader Parameters** section.

3) **Open Hypershade**

   Open the **Windows>Rendering Editors>Hypershade** to manage your shaders and textures.

4) **Create a Map**

   Under the newly created attribute(e.g., color finalColor), click ▽ **Create Map**.

   Set a **Map Resolution** to 10, and **Start Color** to white, then hit **Create**. This will generate a file node (see Figure 1.5.3). Select the file node and from the Attribute Editor(Figure 1.5.4), add a texture image to change the color of your hair.

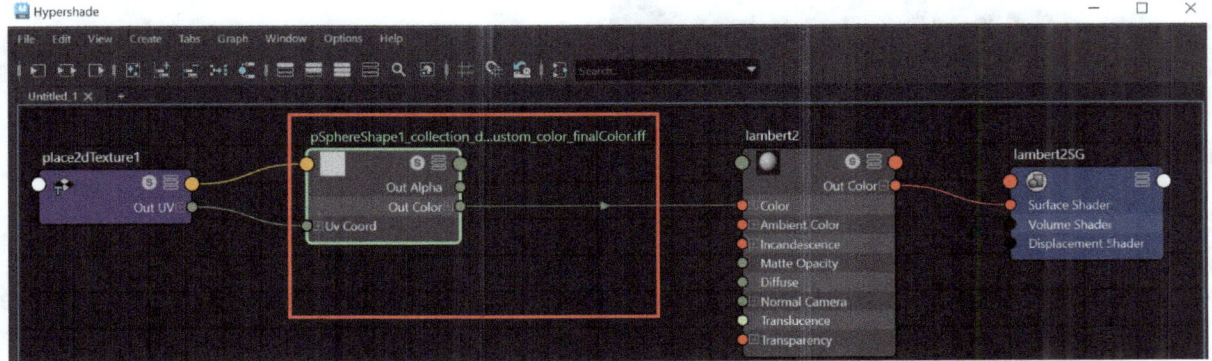

Figure 1.5.3 Adding Textures to Output Settings

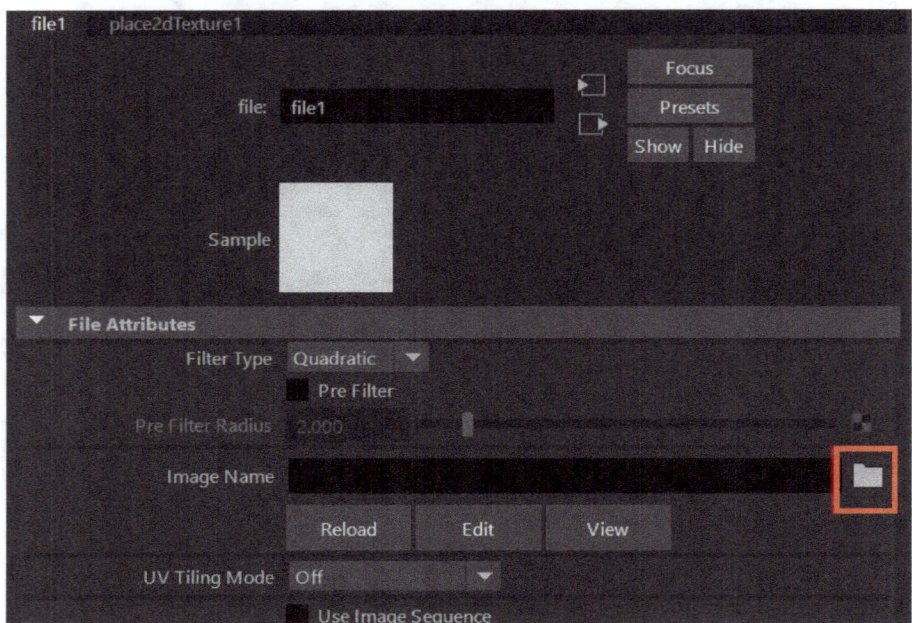

Figure 1.5.4 File Attribute Editor

5) **Create aiUserDataColor Node**

   In Hypershade, press Tab and create an **aiUserDataColor** node. This node will be used to pass color data from the custom shader parameter to the shader network.

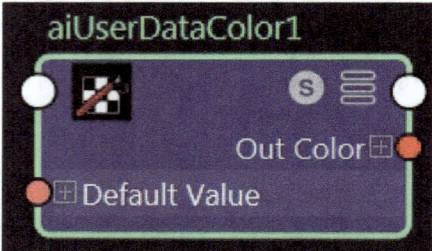

Figure 1.5.5 aiUserDataColor Node

6) **Set the Attribute Name**

   Select the **aiUserDataColor** node and enter the exact same name that you used when creating the custom shader parameter (e.g., finalColor) in the attribute field.

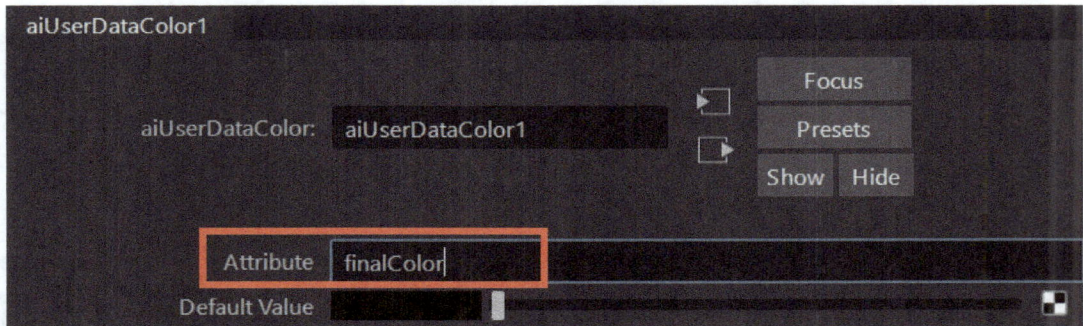

Figure 1.5.6 aiUserDataColor Attribute

7) **Create aiStandardSurface Shader**

   Press tab and create a new shader in **Hypershade**.

   Connect the **aiUserDataColor.outColor** to the base color input of the **aiStandardSurface** shader. This will allow the texture to be used as the base color of the shader.

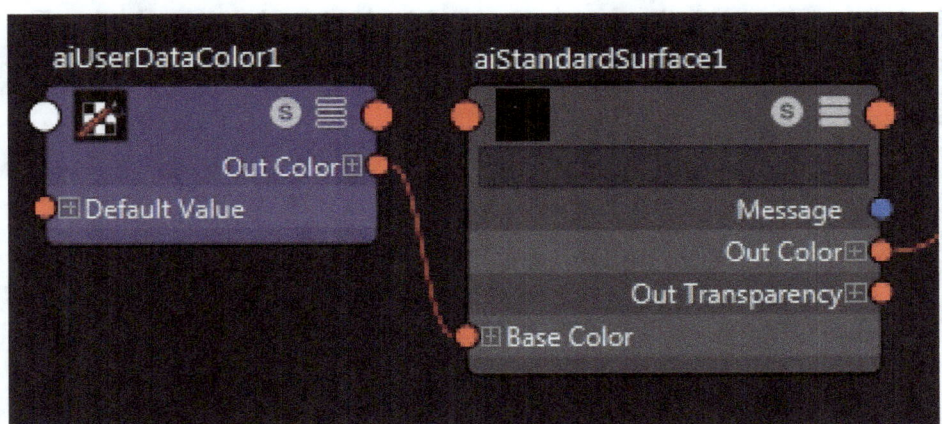

Figure 1.5.7 Connecting to aiStandardSurface

8) **Assign the Shader to the Description Node**

   Select the XGen description node in the Outliner(Figure 1.5.8). Hover the cursor over the aiStandardSurface you just connected, right-click and choose **Assign Material to Viewport Selection**. This will apply the shader to the entire description.

1, Getting Started with XGen Hair Creation

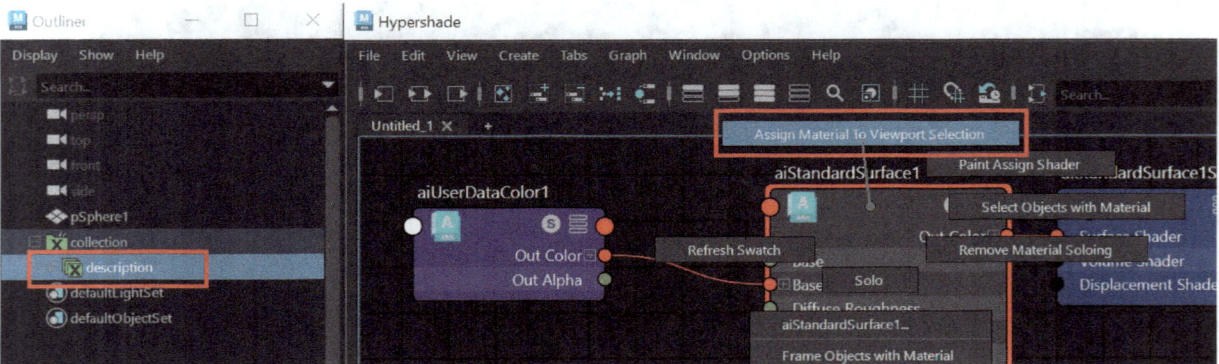

Figure 1.5.8 Assign the Shader to the Description Node

9) **Save**

   Under the **Custom Shader Parameters** section, in the newly created attribute (e.g., color finalColor), press 💾 **Save**. Now your hair should have the texture color applied in the render view. To check this, choose **Arnold>Lights>Skydome Light**. Then, open **Arnold>Open Arnold RenderView**. The texture image should now appear correctly in the render view.

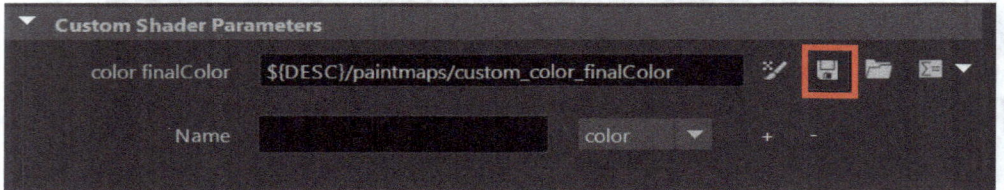

Figure 1.5.9 Custom Shader Parameters

10) **Copy the texture to the Preview Settings**

    To see the hair texture in the viewport, copy the expression 📄 from the **Custom Shader Parameters**(Figure 1.5.10). Paste the script into the **Preview Settings**, **Primitive Color** expressions 📄(Figure 1.5.11), then click the **Apply** button. Press "7" on the keyboard to display all lights in the viewport. Now you should see the viewport texture matching the rendered texture.

XGen Essentials: Long Hair Creation with Splines in Maya

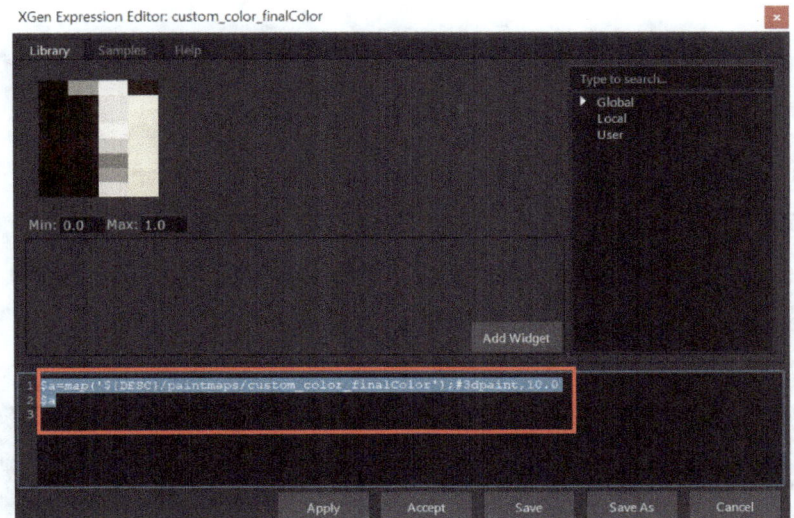

Figure 1.5.10 Copy the Script in XGen Expression Editor

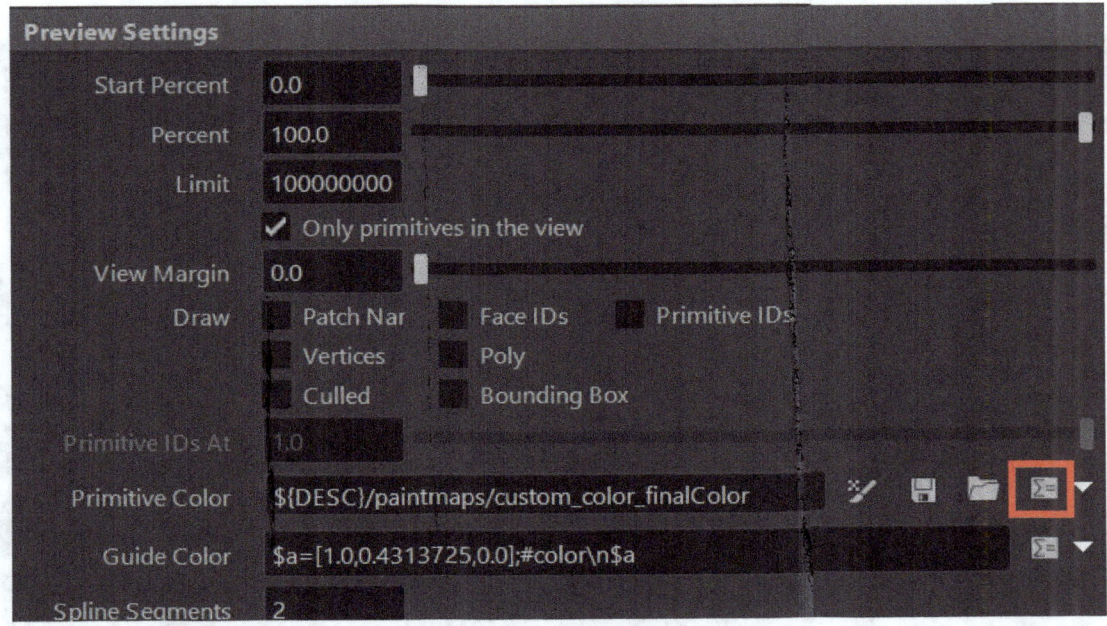

Figure 1.5.11 Paste the Script to Preview Settings

By following these steps, you ensure that your XGen hair or fur will appear correctly in the final render, with the textures and shaders applied as desired.

These settings are vital for controlling how your hair or fur looks both in the viewport and in the final render.

1.6 Modifiers

Modifiers are powerful tools in XGen that allow you to efficiently style and manipulate hair or fur primitives. By adding modifiers, you can quickly achieve complex effects that would be difficult to create manually. In this section, we'll cover the most commonly used modifiers and how to apply them to your XGen description for fast and effective results.

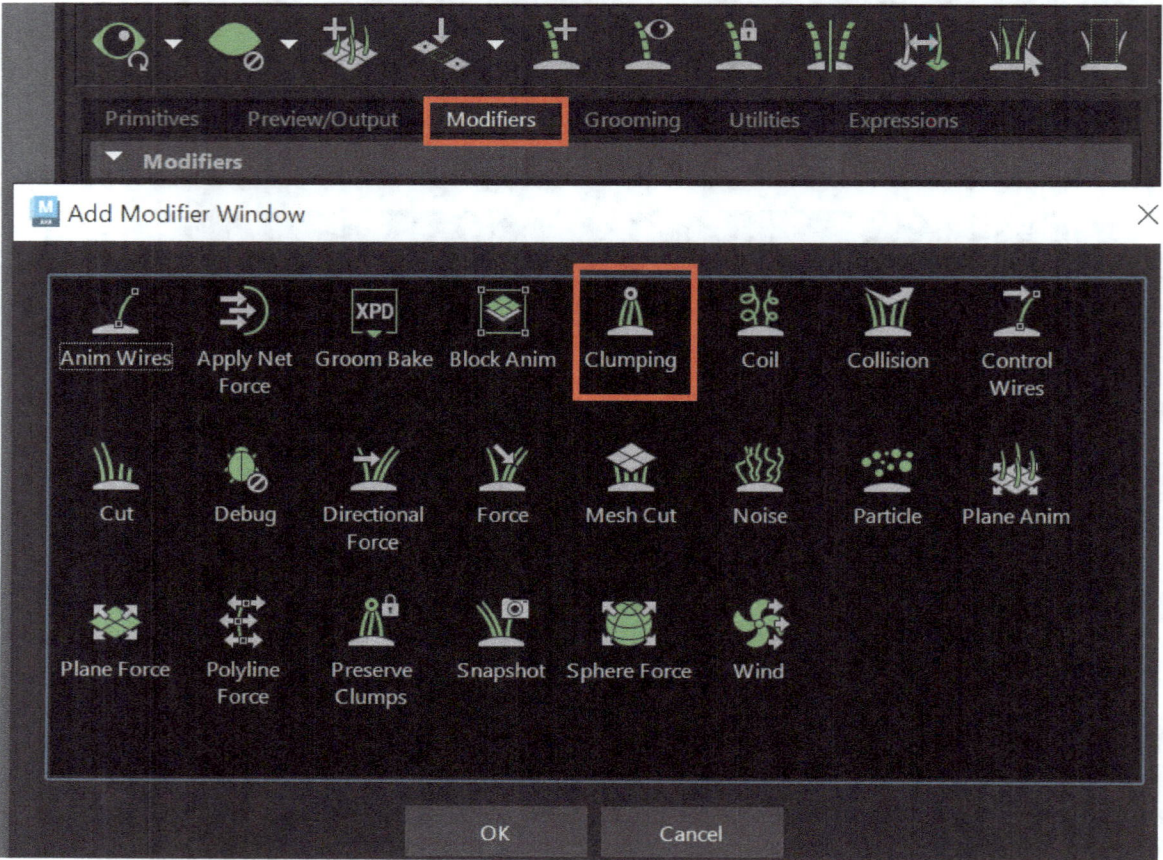

Figure 1.6.1 Modifiers

Clumping Modifier

Clumping is one of the most commonly used modifiers in XGen. It allows you to group primitives into clusters, simulating natural hair behavior, such as clumping together at the roots or tips. This is particularly useful for creating realistic fur or hair effects.

Steps to Set Up Clumping

1) **Add Clump Modifier**

   In the XGen Editor, go to the **Modifiers** tab and press the "Add new modifier" icon on the right. Then add a **Clumping** modifier to your description(Figure 1.6.1).

2) **Setup Clumping Maps**:

   Once the clump modifier is added, click the **Setup Maps** button under the **Curl Effect** to generate the clumping effect(Figure 1.6.2).

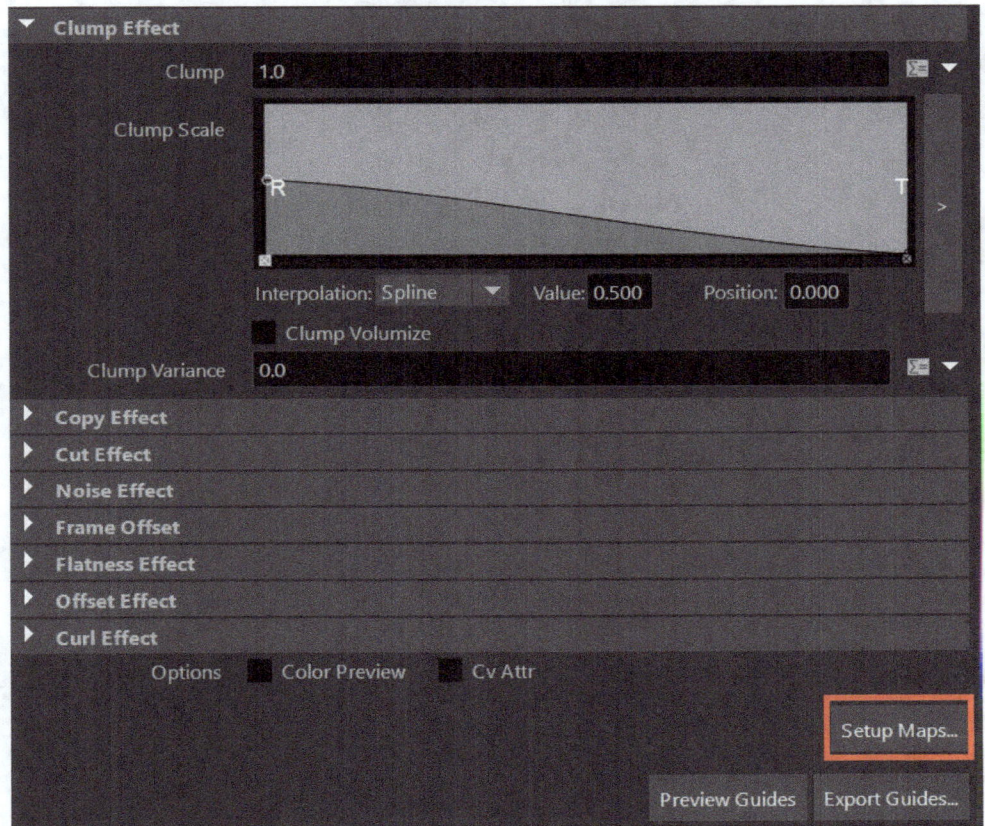

Figure 1.6.2 Clumping Modifiers

-**Clumping Density**

This will open the **Generate Clumping Maps** window, where you can adjust the density of the clumps. The density setting determines how many clumps will be created. Once satisfied, press **Generate**.

1, Getting Started with XGen Hair Creation

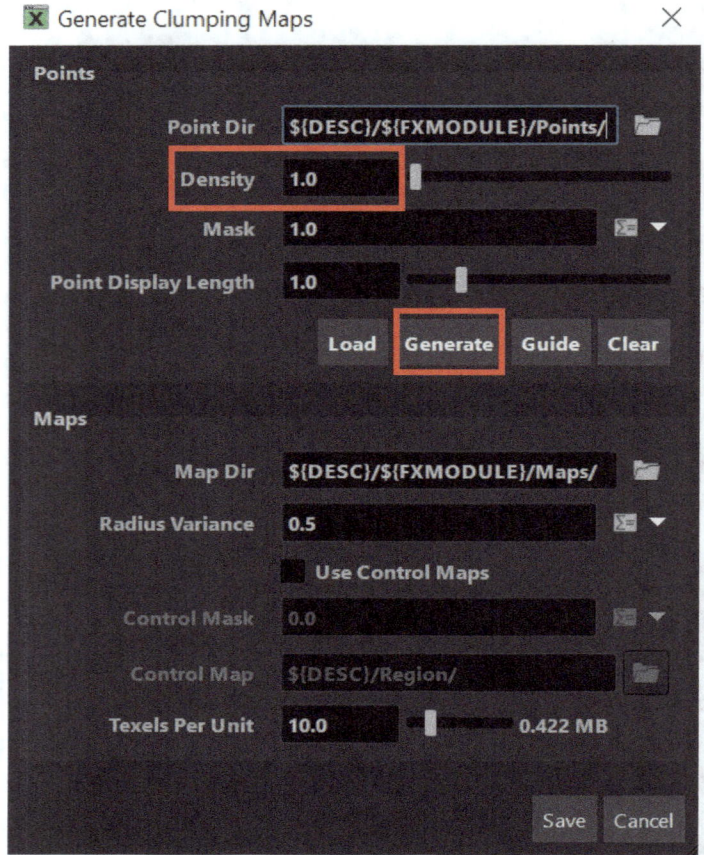

Figure 1.6.3 Generate Clumping Maps

-Clumping on Guides

If you want the clumping to match the guides, press the **Guide** button in **Generate Clumping Maps**. This will create clumps based on the guide shapes, giving you more control over the clumping effect.

3) **Clump Effect**

Play around with the **Clump Scale** Root and **Clump Scale** Tip sliders under **Clump Effect** to adjust the size and shape of the clumps at different points along the hair. You can create larger clumps at the roots and smaller clumps at the tips, or vice versa, depending on the desired style.

Additional Clumping Options
- **Clump Volumize**: This option helps preserve the volume of the hair or fur, preventing clumps from collapsing too much and maintaining a fuller look.

4) Copy Effect > Copy

Adjusts how much the clumps blend with each other. A lower value will cause more blending between clumps, creating a smoother transition.

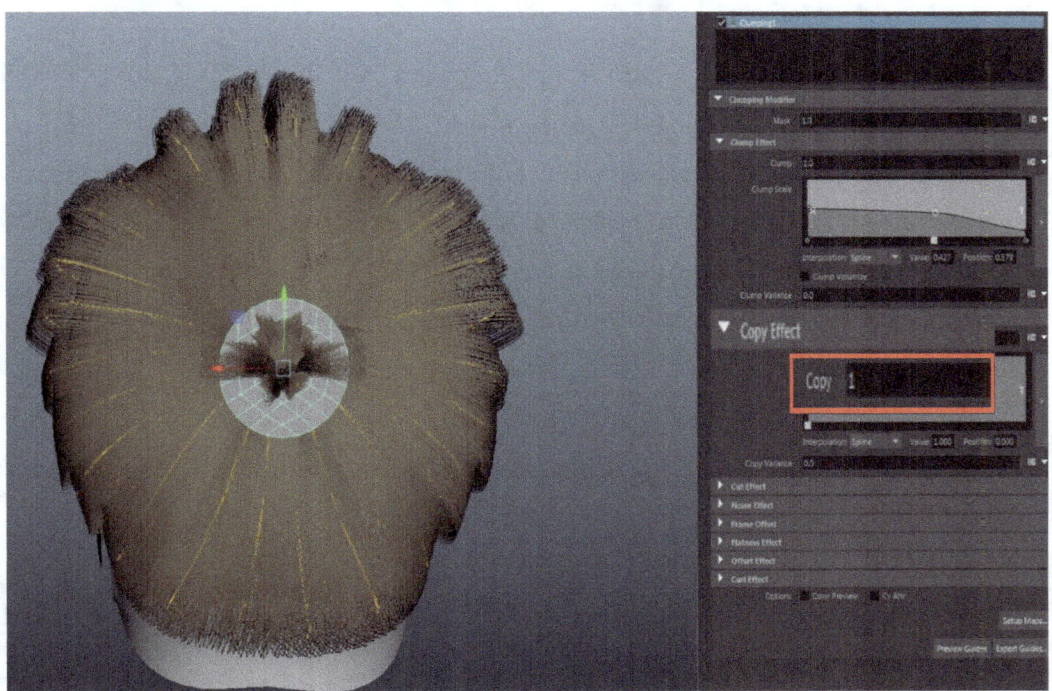

Figure 1.6.4 Copy Effect, Copy:1

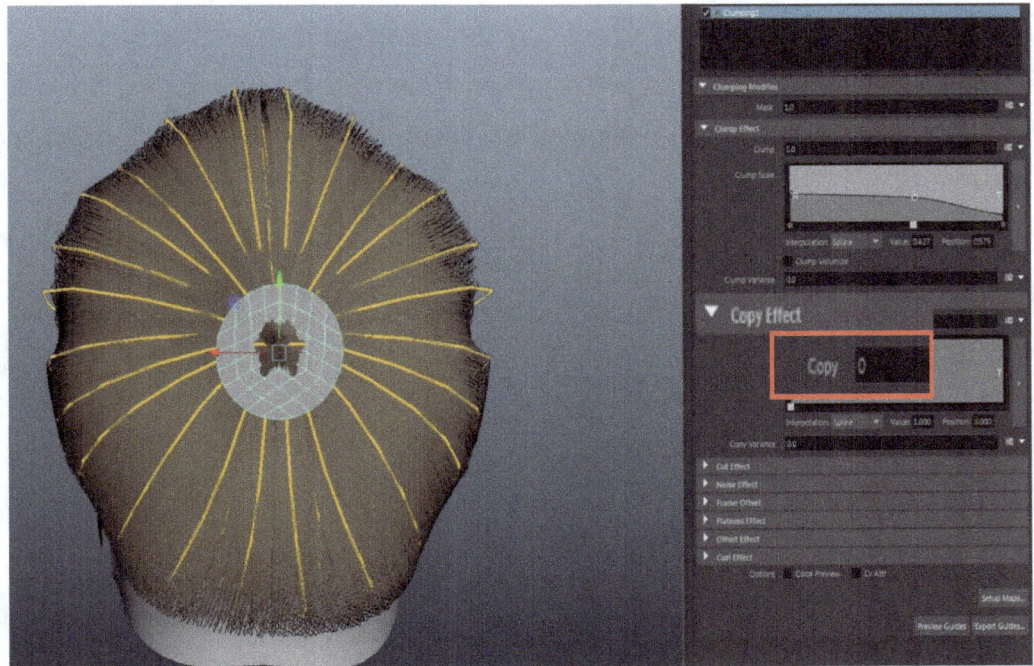

Figure 1.6.5 Copy Effect, Copy:0

5) **Cut Effect:** You can randomly shortens the length of clumps, which can add more variation and realism to your hair or fur.

6) **Noise Effect**: You may need to increase the **Modifier CV Count** in **Primitives** Attributes to properly visualize the noise effect.
    - ✓ **Noise Frequency**: Controls the amount of noise in the primitives. A higher frequency will create more frequent, smaller noise patterns, while a lower frequency will create larger, more sweeping noise patterns.
    - ✓ **Noise Correlation**: Adjusts the offset of noise across the clumps, creating more or less uniformity.

7) **Frame Offset**: Can be used to create a grow effect for the clumps, useful for animations where the hair needs to appear as though it is growing or moving.

8) **Flatness Effect**: Flattens the clumps, making them appear more compressed or less voluminous.

Noise Modifier

The Noise modifier adds randomness and variation to the primitives, creating a more natural, less uniform look. This is particularly useful for simulating frizzy or messy hair, or adding subtle irregularities to fur.

XGen Essentials: Long Hair Creation with Splines in Maya

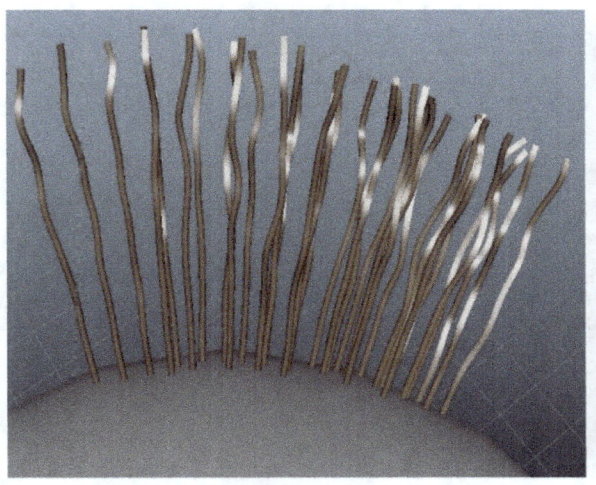 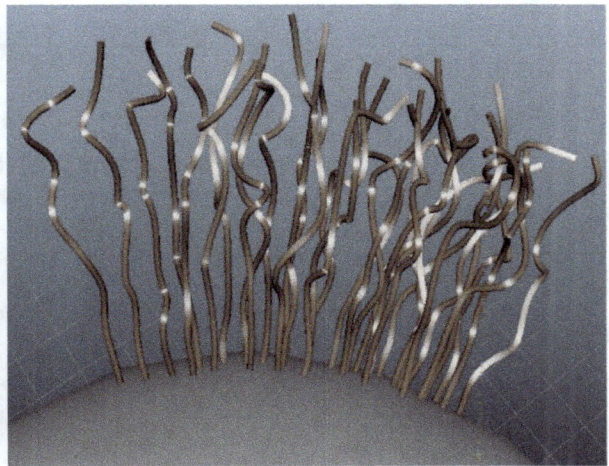

Figure 1.6.6 Compare- Magnitude: 1(left) and Magnitude: 4 (right)

Steps to Set Up Noise

1) **Add Noise Modifier**

   In the **Modifiers** tab, add a **Noise** modifier to your description.

2) **Increase CV Count**

   Before adjusting the noise settings, make sure that the **Mofifier CV Count** in the **Primitives Attribute** is high enough to support the noise effect. More CVs allow for more detailed noise patterns.

3) **Adjust Magnitude**

   Increase the Magnitude setting to make the noise effect more pronounced. A higher magnitude will create more intense randomness, making the hair or fur appear more frizzy or wild.

4) **Fine-Tune the Noise**

   Play with other settings like Frequency to control the scale and position of the noise effect.

Coil Modifier

The Coil modifier creates wavy or curly effects by introducing a spiral or winding pattern to the primitives. This is ideal for creating curly hair, wavy fur, or even natural elements like vines.

1, Getting Started with XGen Hair Creation

Steps to Set Up Coil

1) **Add Coil Modifier**

   In the **Modifiers** tab, add a **Coil** modifier to your description.

2) **Adjust Coil Count**

   The **Count** parameter controls how many times the hair or fur winds around itself. Increasing this value will create tighter curls, while a lower value will create looser waves.

3) **Count Scale**

   Use the Count Scale to control where along the length of the primitive the coiling starts. For example, setting this to 0.5 will begin the coil effect halfway along the primitive.

4) **Radius**

   The Radius parameter (sometimes referred to as Amplitude) controls how wide or strong the coil is. Larger radius values will create bigger, more exaggerated curls, while smaller values will create tighter curls.

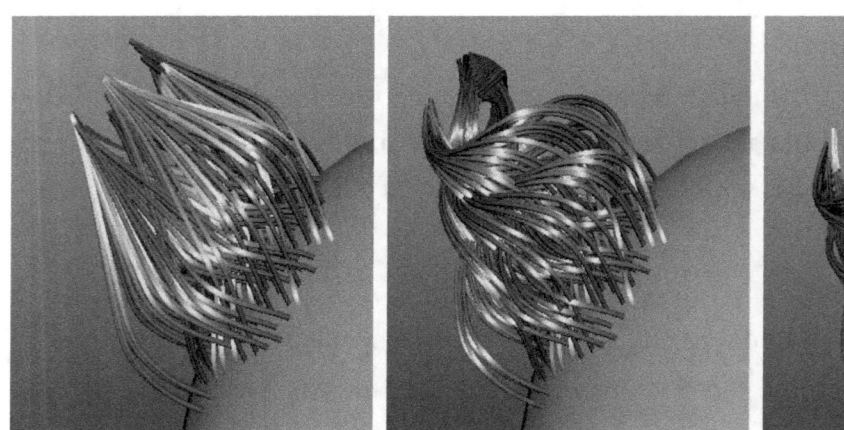

Figure 1.6.7 Count: 0.1, Radius: 1(left) Count: 1, Radius: 1(middle) Count: 1, Radius: 2(right)

Cut Modifier

The Cut modifier trims the tips of the primitives, allowing you to create hair or fur of varying lengths. This is useful for adding variation and realism to your hair, as natural hair often has some strands that are shorter than others.

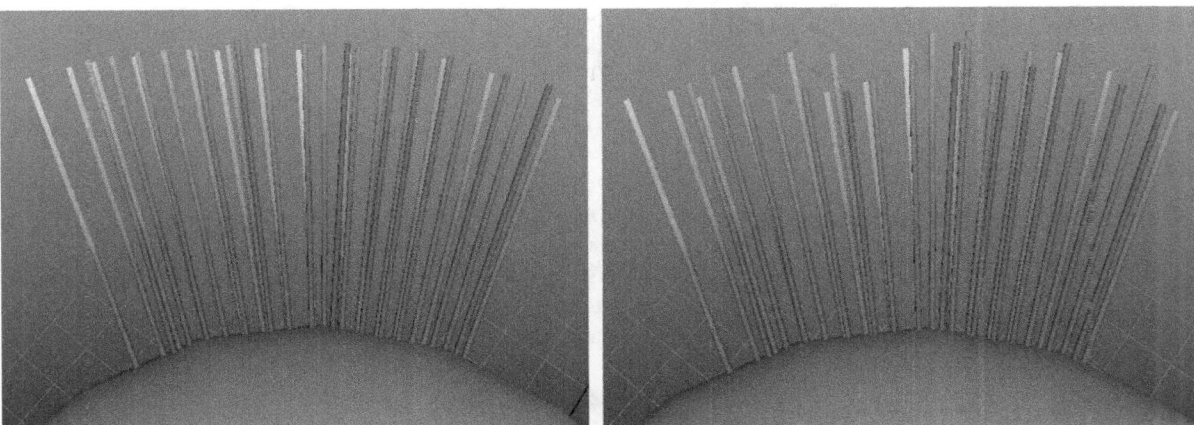

Figure 1.6.8 Amount: 0 (left) and Amount: rand(0.0,1.0) (right)

Steps to Set Up Cut

1) **Add Cut Modifier**

    In the **Modifiers** tab, add a **Cut** modifier to your description.

2) **Adjust Cut Settings**

    The Cut Length setting allows you to specify how much of the primitive should be trimmed. You can apply this uniformly or vary it to create a more natural effect.

3) **Randomize the Cut**

    You can add randomness to the cut lengths to simulate natural variations, where some hair strands are slightly shorter than others by typing "rand(0.0, 1.0)."

With these modifiers, you can quickly and efficiently style your hair and fur primitives in XGen. By combining different modifiers, such as clumping, noise, coil, and cut, you can create a wide range of effects, from sleek and styled hair to wild and messy fur. Experiment with these settings to achieve the look you want, and remember to save your work frequently as you make adjustments.

1.7 Utilities

Utilities in XGen provide additional tools to help shape and manipulate guides and curves, making the hair and fur creation process more flexible and efficient. These utilities allow you to convert between curves and guides, set target guides, and manipulate multiple guides based on a target. In this section, we'll cover the most commonly used utilities.

Curves To Guides

The **Curves To Guides** utility allows you to convert existing curves into XGen guides. This is useful when you've already created curves in Maya and want to use them as guides for shaping hair or fur in XGen.

Steps to Convert Curves to Guides
1) **Select Curves**

    In your Maya scene, select the curves that you want to convert into guides.

2) **Add Guides**

    In the **XGen Editor**, **Utilities** tab, choose **Curves To Guides** and press the **Add Guides button**. This will convert the selected curves into XGen guides, which can now be used to shape your hair or fur.

This utility is particularly helpful when you've modeled specific curve shapes and want to directly apply them to your XGen description.

Guides As Curves

The **Guides As Curves** utility works in reverse of the previous tool, allowing you to convert XGen guides into Maya curves. This is useful if you need to further refine the guide shapes using Maya's curve editing tools or if you want to use the guides for other purposes outside of XGen.

Steps to Convert Guides As Curves
1) **Select Guides**

    Select the guides in your XGen description that you want to convert to curves.

2) **Create Curves**

    In the **XGen Editor**, **Utilites** tab, choose **Guides As Curves** and then press the

Accept button. This will generate new Maya curves based on the selected guides.

This utility is ideal for exporting guide shapes for additional manipulation or for use in other parts of your project.

Target Guide
The Target Guide utility allows you to align other guides to a specific "target" guide. This is helpful when you want multiple guides to follow a similar direction or shape, such as when styling hair in a specific pattern or direction.

Steps to Set a Target Guide
1) **Select the Target Guide**
   Choose the guide that you want to use as the reference for other guides.

2) **Set Target**
   In the **XGen Editor**, **Utilities** tab, choose **Target Guide** to designate the selected guide as the target.

3) **Move Selected Guides**
   Select all the other guides you want to align with the target guide.
   Press the **Move Selected Guides** button. This will cause the selected guides to lean towards and mimic the shape of the target guide.

This utility is very useful for creating uniform hairstyles or fur patterns where multiple strands need to follow a similar flow or direction.

By mastering these utilities, you can streamline your workflow and achieve more precise control over the shape and direction of your XGen hair and fur. These tools are essential for creating complex and detailed hairstyles, fur patterns, or any other XGen-generated elements in your scene.

1.8 Expressions

Expressions in XGen are powerful tools that allow you to create dynamic, customizable hair and fur effects. By using expressions, you can add randomness, control behavior, and fine-tune the appearance of your primitives with precise mathematical operations. The XGen Expression Editor provides a wide range of operators, variables, and functions that you can use to enhance your hair and fur designs.

This section will provide an overview of the key elements of the XGen Expression Editor and a practical example of how to use expressions to add stray hairs with a noise (coil) effect.

Operators, Variables, and Functions in XGen Expressions

Expressions in XGen are built using a combination of operators, variables, and functions. Here's a brief overview of each:

Operators

Operators are symbols that perform operations on variables or values. Some of the most commonly used operators include:

- **Arithmetic Operators**: +, -, *, / (e.g., adding, subtracting, multiplying, and dividing values)
- **Comparison Operators**: >, <, >=, <= (e.g., comparing values to produce a boolean result)
- **Logical Operators**: !x (e.g., logical negation)
- **Conditional Operator**: x?y:z if conditional operator (eg., if x then y else z)

Variables

Variables are placeholders for values that can change. In XGen, you can create your own variables or use built-in ones. Some examples include:

- **$u and $v**: The u and v parameter of the underlying surface
- **$frame**: The current frame in the animation
- **$cWidth**: The width of primitives
- **$cLength**: The length of primitives

You can also create custom variables for specific tasks within an expression.

Functions

Functions perform predefined calculations or operations. XGen provides a variety of functions to help manipulate your hair or fur primitives. Some commonly used functions include:

- **abs()**: Absolute value.
- **rand()**: Generates a random number between 0 and 1.
- **sin(), cos(), tan()**: Trigonometric functions for advanced shape manipulation.
- **length()**: Calculates the length of a vector.
- **norm()**: Normalizes a vector to unit length.

These functions allow you to perform complex operations on your primitives to achieve more natural and varied results.

Example: Adding Noise(Coil) and Stray Hair Using Expressions

One of the common uses of expressions in XGen is to add randomness and variety to hair, such as creating stray hairs. The following example demonstrates how to use an expression to add stray hairs to a coil modifier.

Steps to Add Stray Hair with Noise(Coil) modifier

1) **Apply a Noise (Coil) Modifier**

   First, add a **Noise (Coil)** modifier to your XGen. This will create a base of wavy or curly hair strands.

2) **Access the Mask Setting**

   In the **Noise (Coil)** modifier settings, press the **Mask** expression button . This opens the expression editor, where you can apply an expression to control the stray hair effect.

3) **Write the Expression**

   In the **XGen Expression Editor**, type the following expression:

   $percentStray=5; #0,100
   rand()<$percentStray/100.0 ? 1 : 0

   Explanation:

   $percentStray=5; This line defines a local variable, $percentStray, and sets it to 5. This value represents 5% stray hair, which you can adjust using a slider that ranges from 0 to 100.

   rand()<$percentStray/100.0 ? 1 : 0 This line generates a random value between 0 and 1 using the rand() function. Defined the random value is less than the $percentStray value divided by 100 (to convert it to a percentage), the expression returns 1 if rand()<$percentStray/100.0 is True (indicating that stray hair will be applied). Otherwise, it returns 0 (no stray hair).

4) **Adjust the Stray Hair Percentage**

   After applying the expression, you can slide the mask slider to control the percentage of stray hair. Increasing the percentage will add more stray hairs, while decreasing it will reduce the effect.

This expression-based approach gives you fine control over how stray hairs appear, allowing you to create more natural and varied hair patter

XGen Essentials: Long Hair Creation with Splines in Maya

2. Creating Long Hair with XGen Splines

Figure 2 Referenced from April Rissell and Faylyne

When starting the process of creating long hair with XGen using splines, having a clear reference is essential. For this project, I used hair images by April Rissell and Faylyne as my guide.

Selecting the right reference is more than just choosing an attractive image. It helps you visualize your final result, anticipate challenges, and ensure your style is both achievable and aligned with your vision. A good reference aids in considering factors like complexity, aesthetic appeal, and the practicalities of creation.

In my experience, after exploring various hairstyles online, I found one that perfectly matched my vision. Referencing isn't just about finding a challenging image; it's about making informed choices that balance beauty with technical feasibility.

2.1 Creating a Scalp Geometry

Before diving into XGen for hair creation, it's crucial to establish a clean base geometry for your hair. This is typically done by creating a scalp geometry from your head model. The scalp geometry will serve as the base on which your XGen hair will be applied.

1) **Select the Hair Area**: Start by selecting all the areas on the head where you want the hair to grow. It's better to select slightly more than needed to ensure full coverage.
2) **Duplicate the Geometry**: With the hair area selected, go to **Edit Mesh > Duplicate**. Name the duplicated mesh as "scalp_geo".
3) **Delete History**: Select both the head and the new scalp geometry, then go to **Edit > Delete by Type > History** to remove any construction history that could interfere with the XGen process.

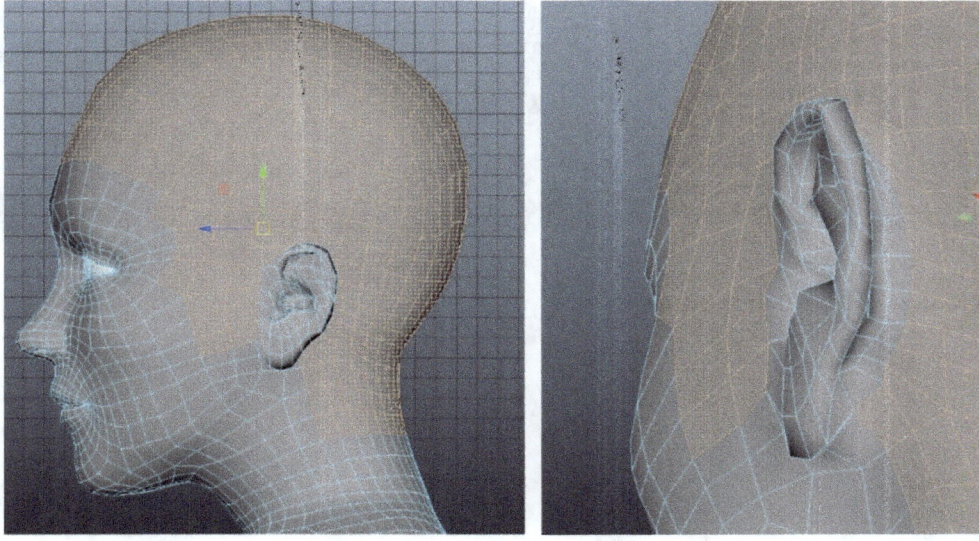

Figure 2.1.1 Creating a Scalp Geometry

2.2 Scalp Geometry UV Mapping

UV mapping is essential for ensuring that your hair textures and effects are applied correctly. Follow these steps to create proper UVs for your scalp geometry.

1) **Planar Mapping**: Select the new geometry(scalp_geo), and in the UV menu, open **UV> Planar** option and set the projection from to the **Z axis**. Apply the planar map, which should project the UVs towards the front of the head.

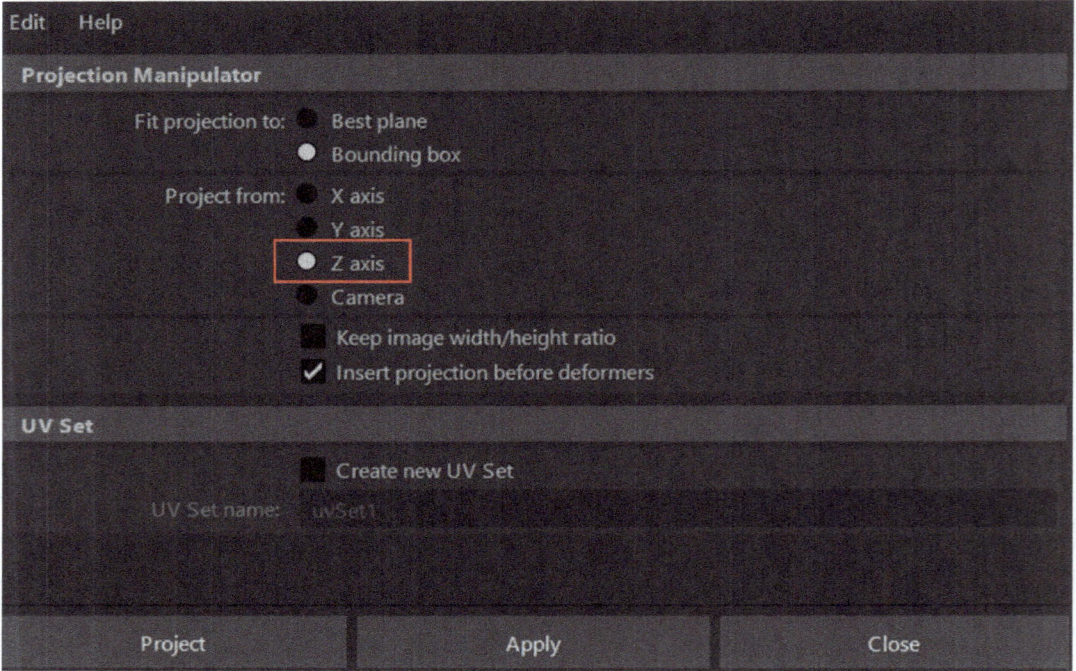

Figure 2.2.1 Planer Mapping

2) **Open the UV Editor**: Go to **UV > UV Editor** to open the UV editor window. Enable the checker map icon (located just below the menu) to help visualize the UV layout.

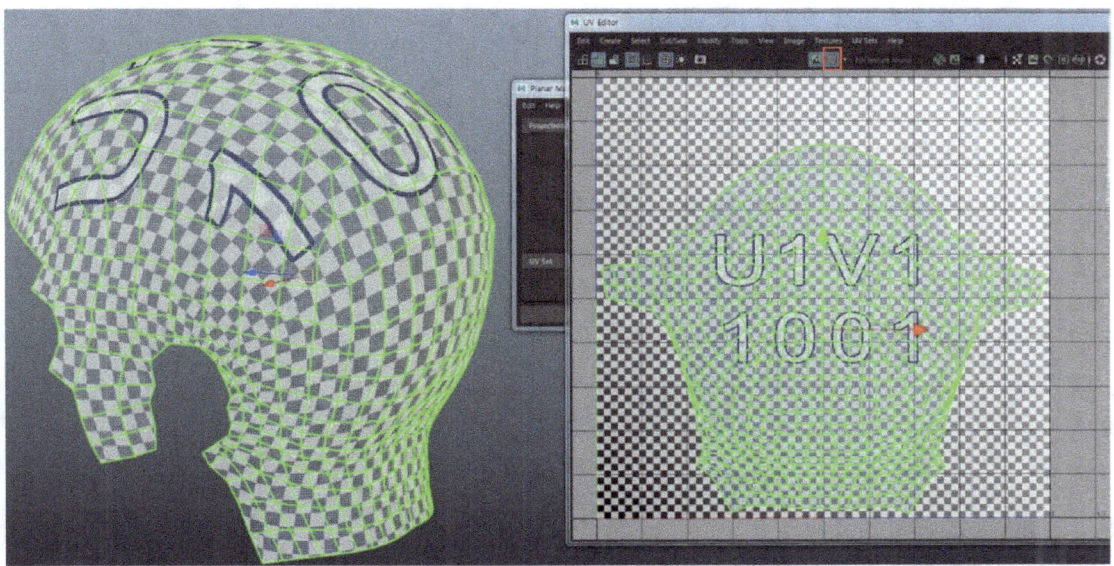

Figure 2.2.2 UV Editor Window

3) **Unfold and Layout UVs**: In the UV Editor, use **Modify > Unfold** to unwrap the UVs, and then use **Modify > Layout** to fit the UVs into the 0-1 UV space. Make sure there are no elongated, stretched, or compressed faces in the UVs by checking with a checker map. Use **UV Editor > Cut/Sew** to cut and sew the UVs in order to spread the scalp more evenly across the plane. Repeat **Modify > Layout** and other tools to refine the UV unwrap and make further adjustments as needed. Rotate the UVs to make them symmetrical(Figure 2.2.2).

2.3 Setting Up Curves for Each Part of the Hair

Before jumping into XGen, it's helpful to plan out the hair design by creating curves that represent the major hair sections. These curves provide a clear understanding of where each hair part will be located.

1) **Create Base Curves**: Start by going to the **side view (Right view)** and create a curve using **Create > Curve Tools > EP Curve Tool**. Begin the curve from the top front of the head. Repeat the process from the **Left view** to define the front part of the hair.

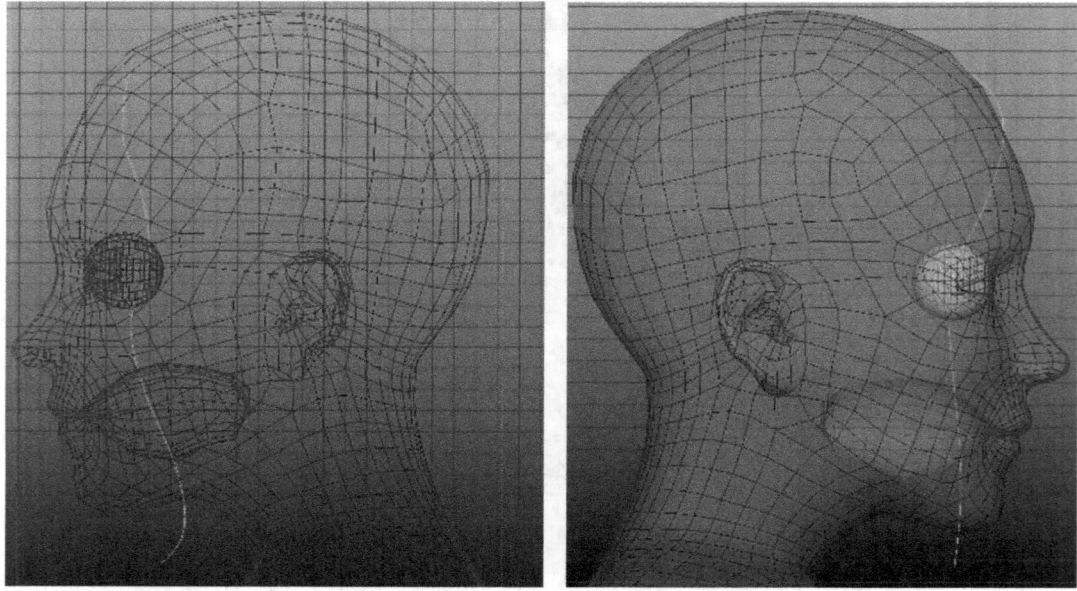

Figure 2.3.1 Creating Base Curves

2) **Adjust Curve Shapes**: Switch to perspective view and adjust the control vertices (CVs) of the curves to refine the hair shape.

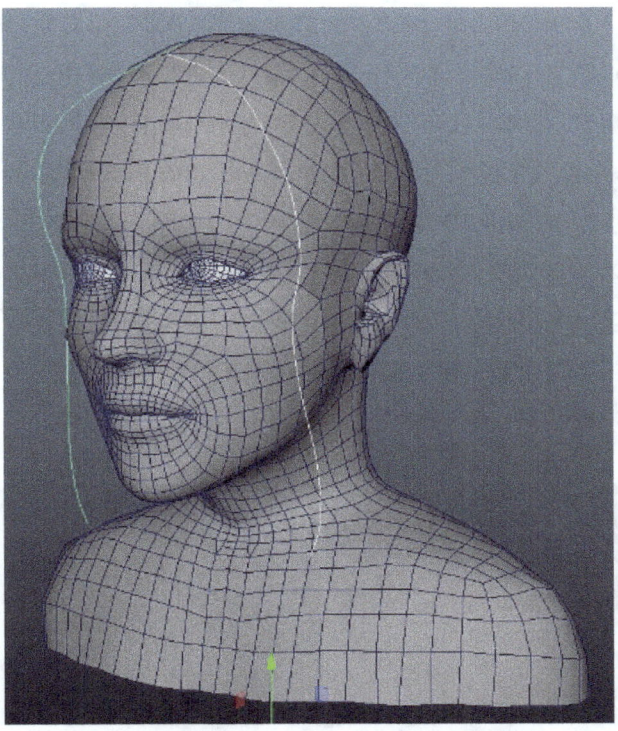

Figure 2.3.2 Adjusting Curve Shapes

3) **Create Wavy Hair Curves**: For wavy or side hair, create additional curves that follow the natural flow of the hair. Always start from the root and move towards the tip. You can enable **Make Live** for the scalp geometry to ensure that the curves adhere to the scalp surface. To enable this, select the scalp geo and go to **Modify > Make Live**. If you want to turn off object live mode, simply disable the object live button.

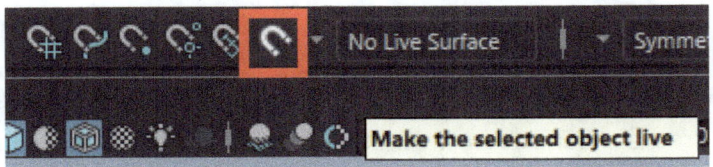

Figure 2.3.3 Make the Selected Object Live

4) **Create Spiral and Bun Shapes**: For more complex hairstyles like buns or spirals, you can try using spiral geometries to trace your curve. If you don't have spiral geometries, start by creating the curve in the side view, then switch to the perspective view to achieve the desired three-dimensional shape. These curves will serve as a guide for more detailed work in XGen. Designing hair shapes using curves is a skill that develops through extensive experience. You need to rotate the curves in 3D space, carefully observing them from different angles while considering aesthetic positioning. While you are welcome to closely replicate the curves I've created, I recommend that you also experiment with your own style to naturally shape the hair.

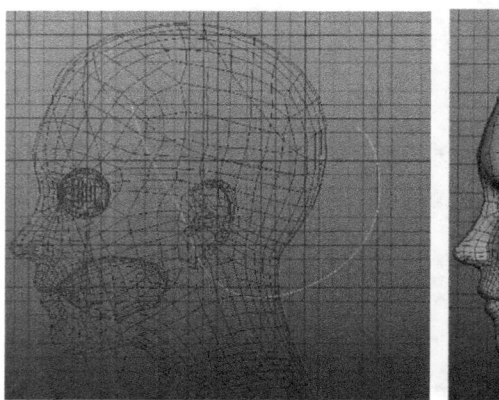 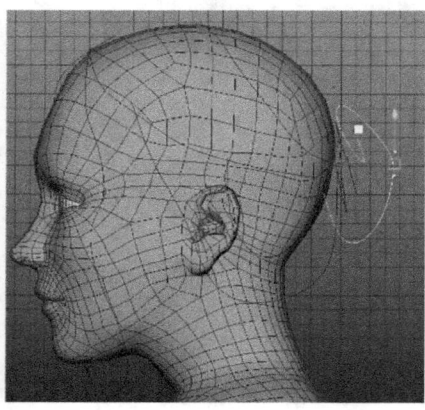 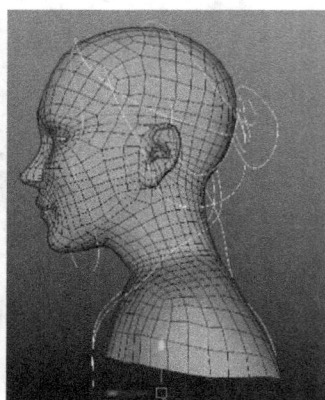

Figure 2.3.4 Creating Spiral and Bun Shapes

2.4 Simple Surface Generation

Once you've laid out the curves, you can generate simple surfaces to get a rough idea of the hair layout.

1) **Loft Curves**: Select two curves that represent sides shape of a hair section and go to **Surfaces > Loft**. This will create a surface between the curves, giving you a visual representation of the hair volume.

XGen Essentials: Long Hair Creation with Splines in Maya

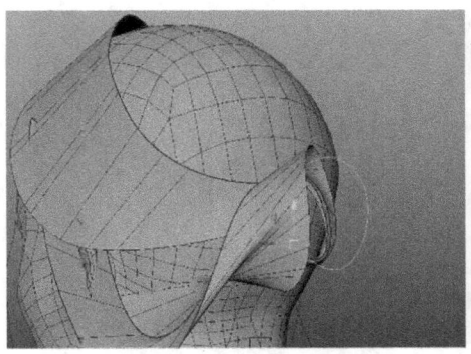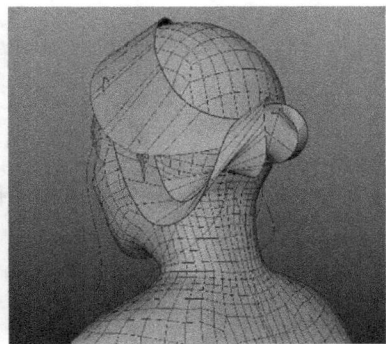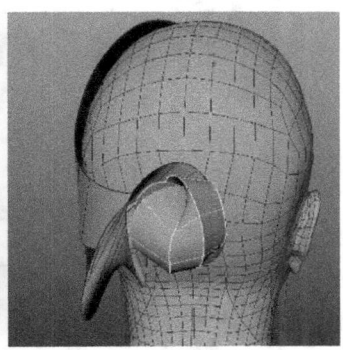

Figure 2.4.1 Loft Curves

2) **Adjust Lighting**: If the surface appears black, enable **Two Sided Lighting** from the Lighting menu in the viewport's toolbar to ensure both sides of the surface are properly lit.

3) **Check Proportions**: Make any necessary adjustments to the curves, and the surface will automatically update. This step allows you to refine the overall proportions before diving into detailed hair creation.

2.5 Duplicating and Mirroring Curves

After creating the left side of the hair, you can easily mirror the curves to create the right side.

1) **Duplicate Curves**: Select all the curves on the left side and duplicate them (**Ctrl+D**).
2) **Group and Mirror**: Group the duplicated curves (**Ctrl+G**) and set the group's scale in the X-axis to **-1** to mirror them to the right side.
3) **Adjust Right Side Curves**: After mirroring, adjust the CVs of the right side curves to create a more natural hair shape.

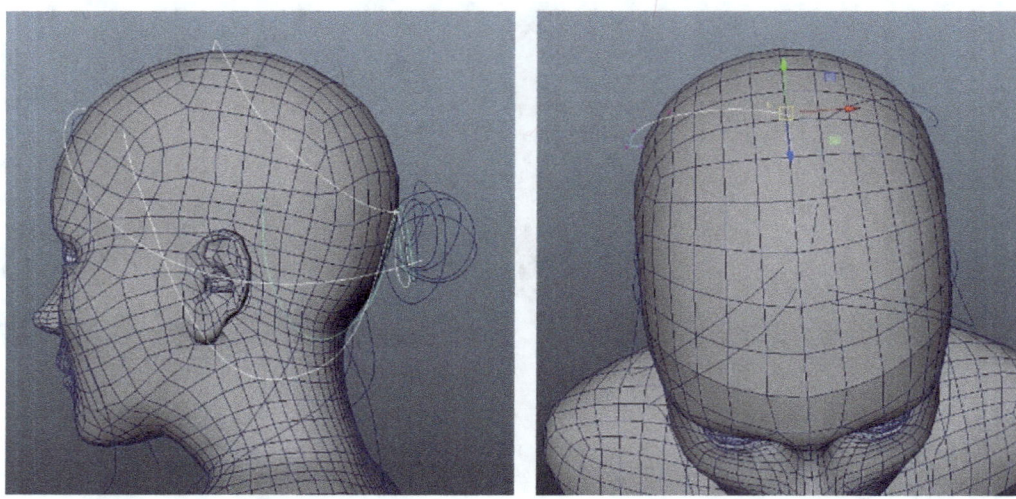

Figure 2.5.1 Adjusting Right Side Curves

2.6 Finalizing Curves

If any of the curves require refinement, especially for complex shapes like spirals, you can edit or cut them as needed.

1) **Detach Curves**: To cut a section of a curve, right-click on the curve and select **Curve Points**. Click where you want the cut to occur, then go to **Curves > Detach** to split the curve into two parts.

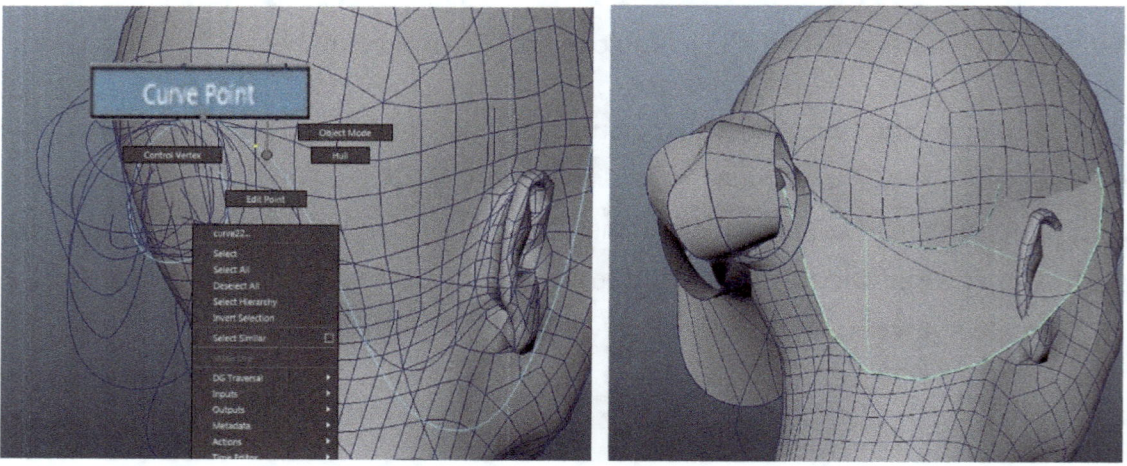

Figure 2.6.1 Detach Curves

2) **Delete Unnecessary Sections**: Once the curve is detached, delete any unnecessary sections, such as extra spiral shapes.

By following these steps, you will have a well-planned set of curves that define the overall structure of the hair. Setting up a well deformed curve shape is crucial and will make the process of generating long hair in XGen much smoother and more controlled. In the next chapter, we will explore how to use these curves to create detailed guide curves and begin the process of generating realistic long hair using XGen's splines system.

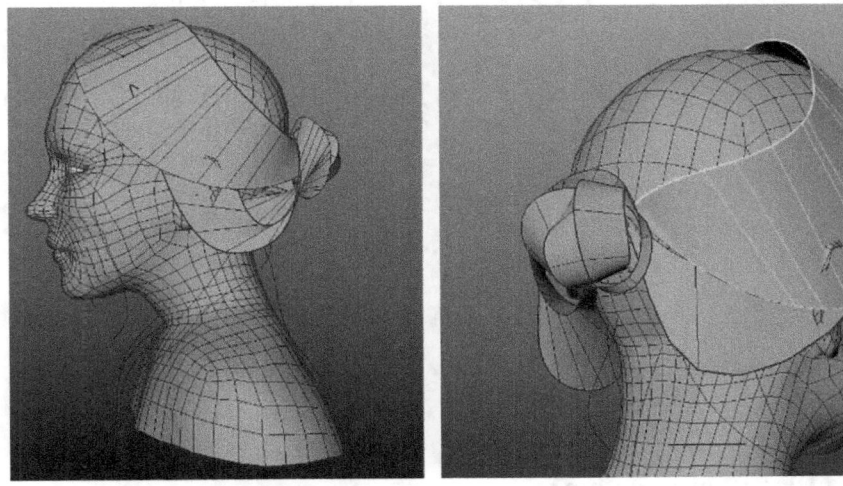

Figure 2.6.2 Final Curve Shapes

XGen Essentials: Long Hair Creation with Splines in Maya

3. Shaping Hair Layers for Realism

Figure 3 Referenced from April Rissell and Faylyne

3.1 Creating Top Hair

Creating Curves for the Top Hair

In this chapter, we'll guide you through the process of creating and styling the top section of hair using XGen. This includes setting up curves to define the hair shape, generating guides, and applying modifiers for a more detailed and refined output.

XGen Essentials: Long Hair Creation with Splines in Maya

Set the Scalp Geometry to Live

1) **Select the Scalp Geometry**: In the **Outliner**, select your scalp_geo object.
2) **Set Object to Live**: To make the scalp surface "live" and allow curves to stick to it, go to **Modify > Make Live**.

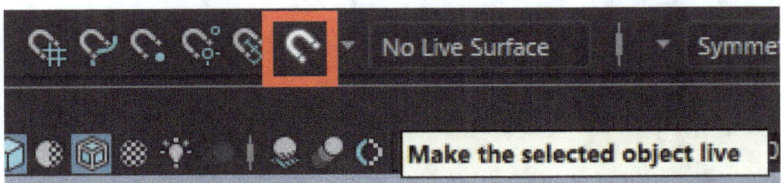

Figure 3.1.1 Make the Selected Object Live

Create Curves on the Scalp

1) **Open the EP Curve Tool**: Go to **Create > Curve Tools > EP Curve Tool**.
2) **Draw Curves on the Scalp**: Create curves on the top part of the **scalp_geo** object. Aim to cover the entire upper surface area with curves, which will form the base of the hair. For this example, we create five layers of curves, ranging from long to short. The more curves you create, the better the final output will be.

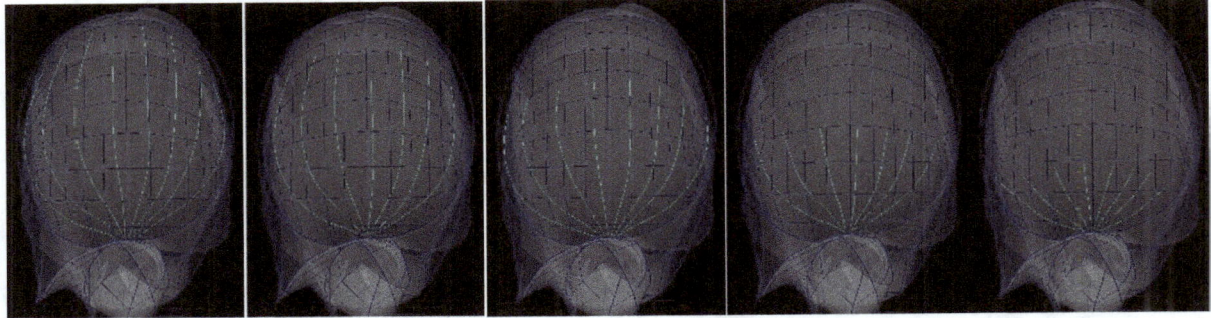

Figure 3.1.2 Five Layers of Curves, Ranging From Long to Short

3) **Evenly Space the Curves**: Make sure the starting points of the curves are evenly spaced across the scalp to create a consistent and natural look.

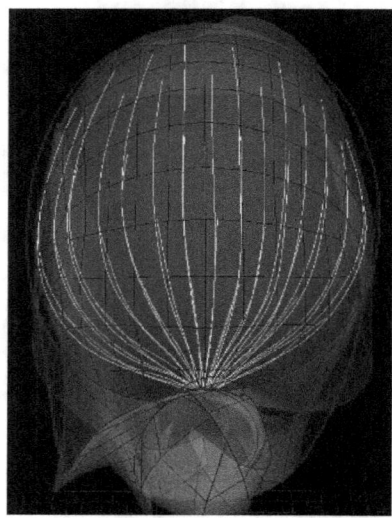

Figure 3.1.3 Evenly Space the Curves

Adjusting the Curves to Create Volume

Once the curves are created, we need to manipulate them to give the hair volume and flow.

1) **Disable Make Live**: Select the scalp_geo object in the Outliner again and disable the **Make Live** option. This allows you to freely manipulate the curves without them sticking to the scalp.
2) **Select the Last CV of Each Curve**: Choose all the curves you created, then go to **Select > Last CV**. This will select the last control vertex (CV) of each curve.
3) **Scale Down the Ends**: Scale down the selected CVs until the ends of all the curves converge in a single area. Then, switch to the **Right view** and move the end points of the curves to the right, where the bun or other hairstyle begins (Figure 3.1.4 left).

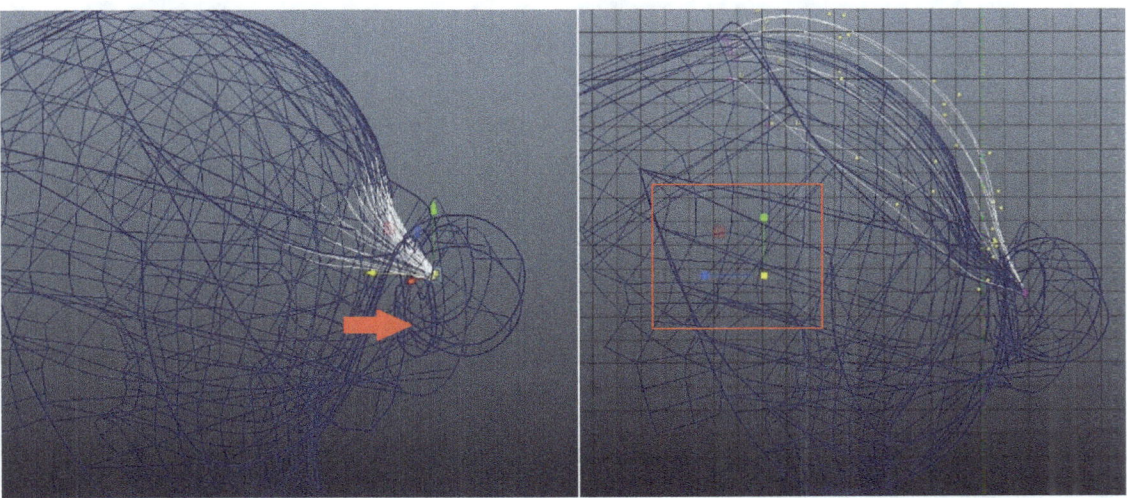

Figure 3.1.4 Shaping the Curves

4) **Create Volume**: Select all the CVs on the curves except the first and last ones. Hold down the **D** key to move the pivot point to the center of the head. Scale up the curves to add volume to the top hair (Figure 3.1.4 right).

Finalizing the Curves

After adjusting the curves, your top hair setup should now have a realistic volume and shape. These curves will form the basis for the hair guides in XGen.

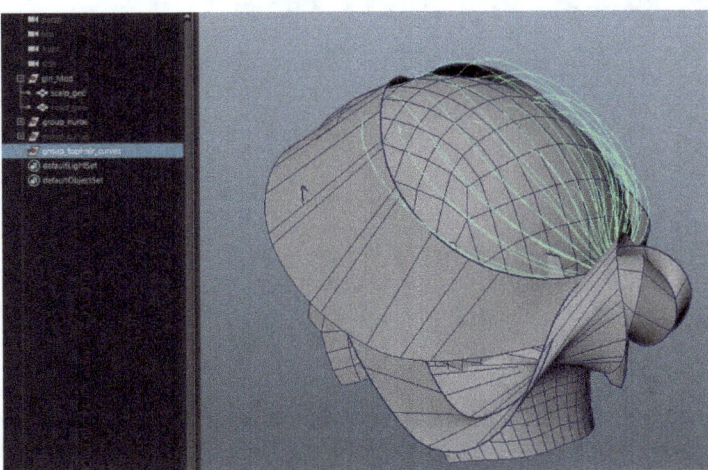

Figure 3.1.5 Final Top Curves

3. Shaping Each Hair Layer

Generating Top Hair in XGen

Now that the curves are in place, it's time to generate the hair using XGen.

Create a New XGen Description

1) **Select the Scalp Geometry**: Select the scalp_geo object again.
2) **Create a New Description**: Go to **Generate > Create Description** to start a new XGen description.
3) **Set Description and Collection Names**: Name the description topHair_description and set the collection name as Female_collection.
4) **Choose Hair Type**: Select **Splines (use for long hair)**, **Randomly across the surface**, **Placing and shaping Guides**.

Convert Curves To Guides

1) **Select All Curves**: Select all the top hair curves that you created earlier.
2) **Use Curves to Guides**: Under the **XGen Utilities** tab, select **Curves To Guides**. Make sure to uncheck the **Delete Curves** options, then press the **Add Guides** button.

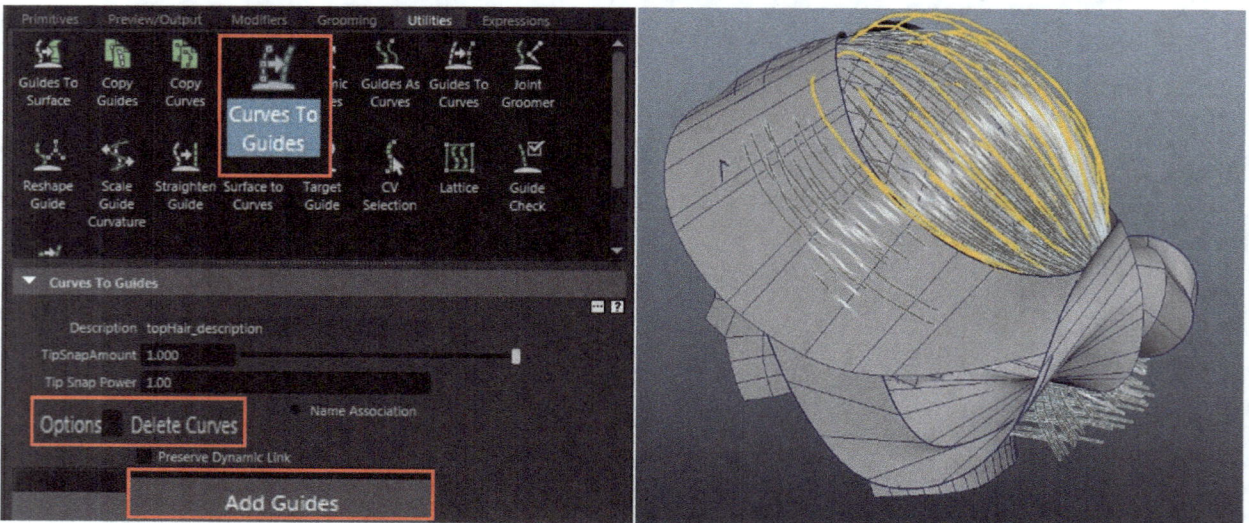

Figure 3.1.6 Convert Curves To Guides

3) **Check the Generated Guides**: Guides based on your curves should now be created on the scalp geometry.

Create and Apply a Mask Map

1) **Open the Primitives Tab**: Under the **Primitives** tab, **Generator Attributes** click the down arrow ▽ located on the right side of the **Mask** attribute.

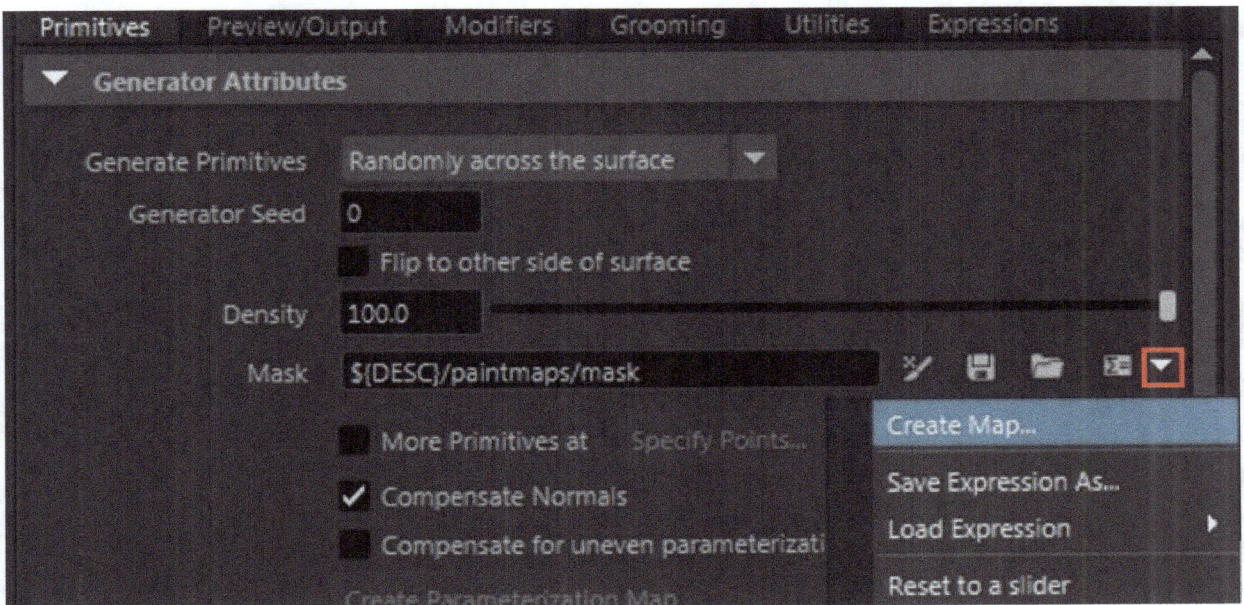

Figure 3.1.7 Apply Mask

2) **Create a New Mask Map**: Click on the ▽ **Create Map** button for the mask. Set the map resolution to 100 and the start color to Black, then press **Create**.
3) **Paint the Top Hair Area**: Using the 3D paint tool, paint the top hair area with white to define the active region where the hair will grow. Ensure you are using a hard brush rather than a soft one for precision (Figure 3.1.8).

3. Shaping Each Hair Layer

Figure 3.1.8 Choose Hard Brush

Tip: In the 3D Paint Tool's **Tool Settings**, under **Stroke**, turn on **Reflection** to simultaneously paint the other side in the -X direction.

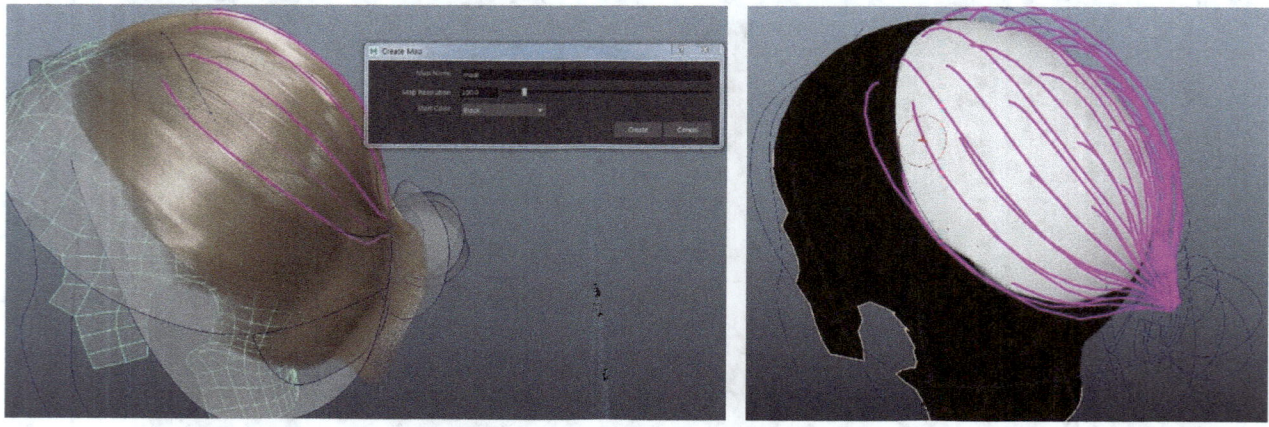

Figure 3.1.9 3D Paint Tool

4) **Save the Mask**: Once you've finished painting the mask, press the **Save** icon next to the Mask Attribute to save the map.

Applying Modifiers to Refine the Hair

XGen Essentials: Long Hair Creation with Splines in Maya

To enhance the realism of your top hair, you'll need to apply modifiers. The most commonly used modifier for hair is the **Clumping Modifier**, which helps to group hair strands together and add natural variation. I will cover only the simple steps for modifiers for now and explain more details in Chapter 4: Applying Modifiers in XGen.

1) **Add Clumping Modifiers**

   Apply Clumping Modifier: After setting up the guides, add a **Clumping Modifier** to your XGen description. This will help you achieve a more realistic, clustered look for the top hair.

2) **Refining and Previewing**

   Before adding further details and refinements, it's a good idea to preview how the hair looks with the initial clumping modifier applied.

At this stage, your top hair should be taking shape. Continue refining the guides and applying modifiers as needed to achieve the final look.

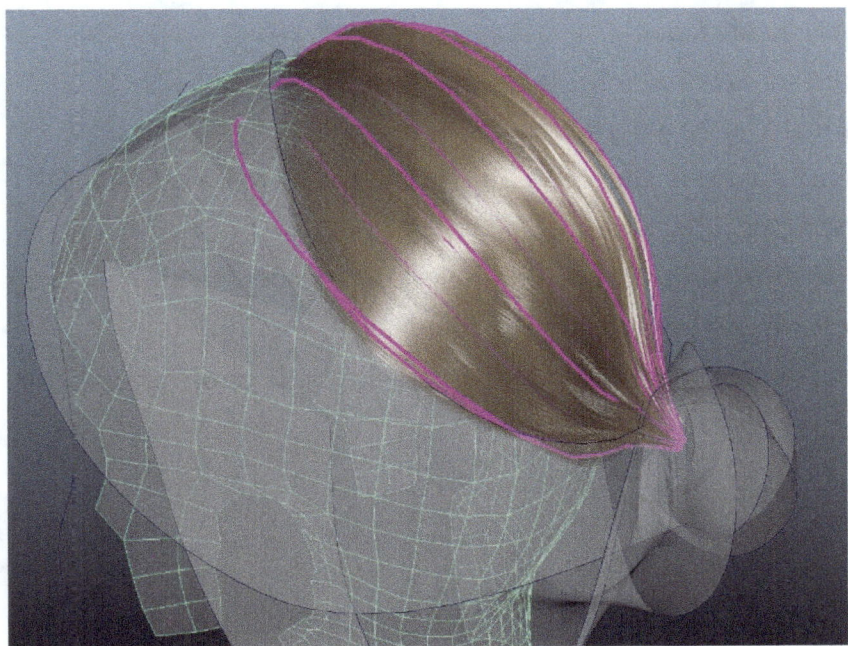

Figure 3.1.10 adding a Clump Modifier

3. Shaping Each Hair Layer

3.2 Creating Braid Hair

We will explore efficient methods to create braid hair in XGen. While manually sculpting braid guide curves can be challenging, we'll introduce techniques that simplify the process and help achieve realistic results.

Creating Braid Geometry

Before diving into XGen, we will first create the underlying braid geometry, which will serve as the foundation for generating hair.

Creating Curves

1) **Front View Setup**: Switch to the Front view and create a curve using **Create > Curve Tools > EP Curve Tool**. Start at coordinates (0,0,0) and extend the curve to (0,40,0).
2) **Rebuild the Curve**: Go to **Curves > Rebuild Option** and set the **Number of spans** to 20. Press **Rebuild** to apply the changes.
3) **Create a Cylinder**: Create a cylinder and set its height to 40, subdivision height to 80, and position it with Translate Y at 20. Adjust the cylinder radius to 0.5.
4) **Delete History**: With the cylinder selected, go to **Edit > Delete by Type > History** to clean up any construction history.
5) **Apply Wire Deform**: Choose **Deform > Wire**. First, select the cylinder, press enter, then select the curve, and press enter again to apply the deformer.
6) **Adjust Dropoff Distance**: Select the wire deformer and adjust the **Dropoff Distance** to 100.

XGen Essentials: Long Hair Creation with Splines in Maya

Figure 3.2.1 Wire Deformer Dropoff Distance to 100

7) **Hide the Cylinder**: Hide the cylinder by pressing **Ctrl+H**.
8) **Manipulate CVs**: Select a pair of CVs, skip the next two, and repeat this process along the curve, and move them one unit to the left, and select the other pair of CVs and move one unit to the right using grid snap (**X + LMB**). Check Figure 2.3.2(a).
9) **Adjust CVs in Side View**: In the Side view, select every other CV Figure 2.3.2(b) and move them 2 units to the right, then move the other CVs 2 units to the left to create a braid pattern Figure 2.3.2(c).

3. Shaping Each Hair Layer

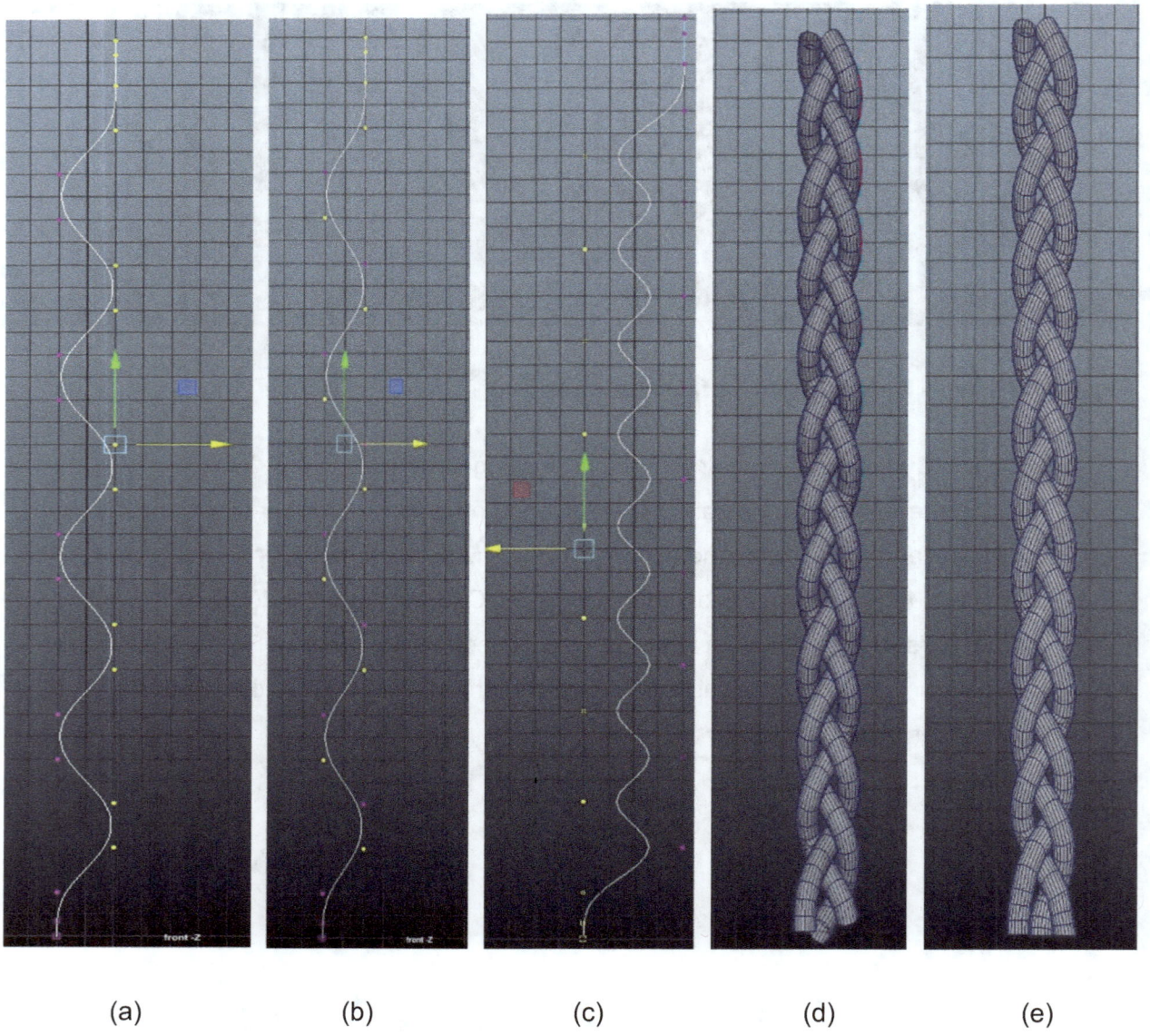

(a)　　　　(b)　　　　(c)　　　　(d)　　　　(e)

Figure 3.2.2 Creating Braid Geometry

Refining the Braid Geometry

1) **Unhide the Cylinder**: Bring the cylinder back by pressing **Shift+H**.
2) **Duplicate the Cylinder**: Duplicate the cylinder and set Translate Y to 22.5 for the first duplicate, and 25 for the second duplicate Figure 3.2.2(d).

3) **Trim Unnecessary Faces**: Select the top and bottom faces of the cylinders and delete any unnecessary parts Figure 3.2.2(e).
4) **Refine the Shape**: Adjust the top and bottom areas as needed, keeping in mind that the bottom will serve as the braid's root.
5) **Combine the Cylinders**: Select all three cylinders and go to **Mesh > Combine** to merge them into a single geometry.
6) **Scale the Braid**: Scale it thinner in the Side view to give the braid a thinner profile.
7) **Clean Up Geometry**: Select the combined geometry and go to **Edit > Delete by Type > History**, then apply **Modify > Freeze Transformations** to reset transformations.
8) **Name the Geometry**: Rename the combined geometry as braid_geo.

Adding a Deformer

With the braid geometry in place, the next step is to add a deformer and joints to shape and position the braid.

Applying the Flare Deformer

1) **Apply Flare Deformer**: Select the braid_geo and go to **Deform > Nonlinear > Flare**.
2) **Adjust Flare Attributes**: Set **Start Flare X** and **Z** to 1.9, **End Flare X** and **Z** to 0, and **Curve** to 0.3. Adjust these values as needed based on the hairstyle.

Creating Joints and Binding Skin

1) **Create Joints**: Go to **Skeleton > Create Joints** and create joints from the bottom of the braid, adding a joint every 4 units up to the top.
2) **Bind Skin**: Select the first joint, then go to **Skin > Bind Skin** and press **Apply**. Reset the Bind Skin options before applying.
3) **Position the Braid**: Select the first joint and place it on the scalp_geo and adjust the joint and flare attributes to ensure proper positioning of the braid.

4) **Duplicate the Braid Geometry**: Once the braid is positioned correctly, duplicate the braid_geo and rename it braidLeft_geo.
5) **Group and Hide**: Group the joint, braid_geo, curve, and flare handle, then name the group as groupDeformGeo. Hide this group (using **Shift+H**) as it won't be used for now. You can later duplicate this for the opposite side of the braid.

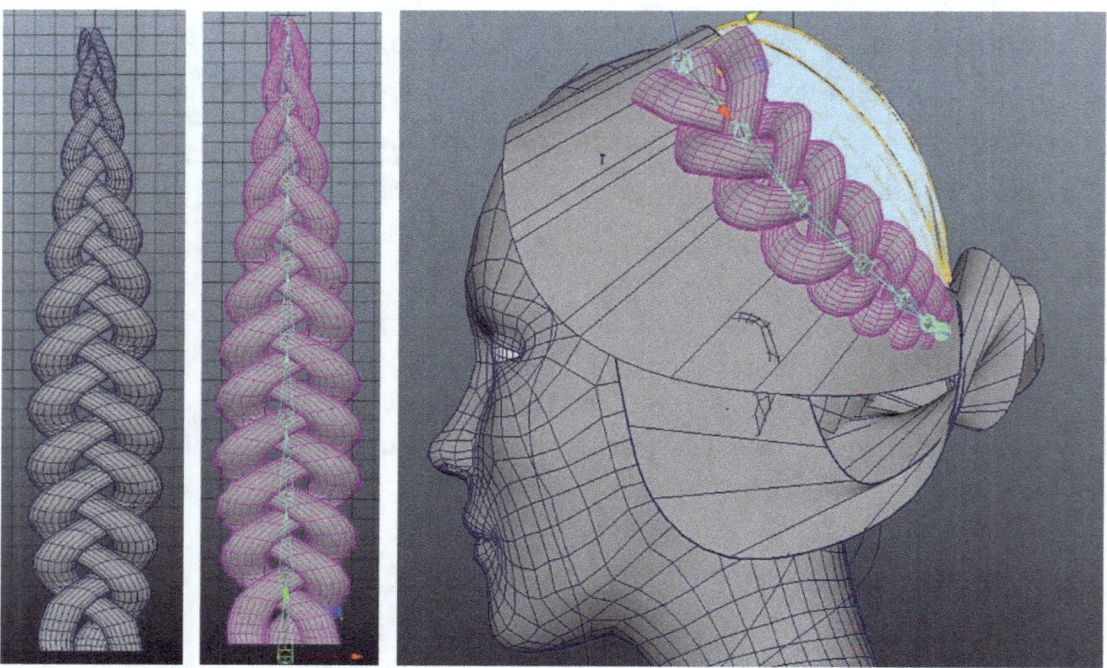

Figure 3.2.3 Shaping with Joints

Adjusting the Braid to Fit the Scalp

1) **Align Vertices**: Select the starting vertices of braidLeft_geo and align them to the scalp_geo. If the root and tip of a polygon (braidLeft_geo) are blocked, you may want to delete faces to open them up. Adjust and delete extra faces as needed to match the shape.
2) **Choose a Method**: You have two options for creating the top braid hair: Figure 3.2.4 (left) Shape the braid geometry all the way to the top, or Figure 3.2.4 (right) create a separate layer (description) for the top area and connect the two. The second method

offers more flexibility and control, making it easier to manage the hair. I will explain how to set up the second method soon in the section "Creating the Top Braid Hair."

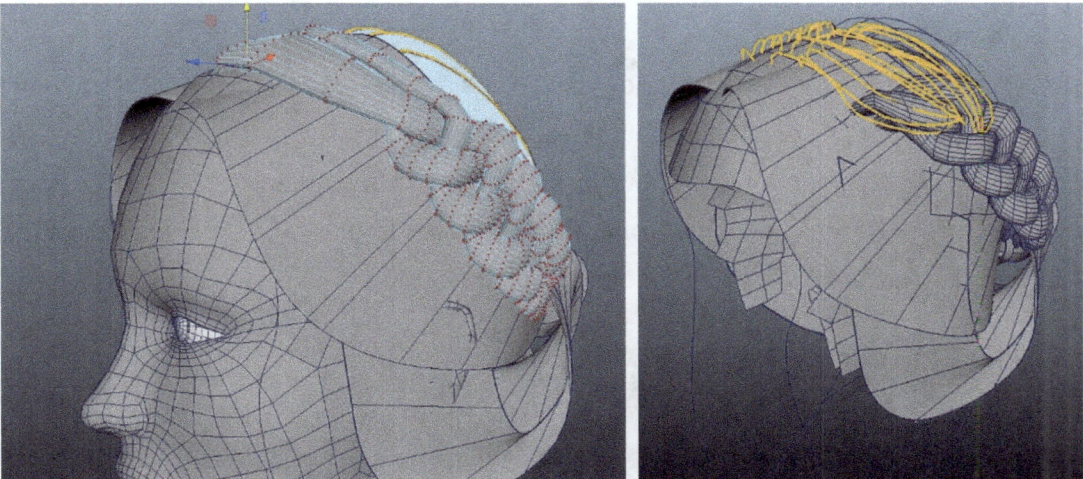

Figure 3.2.4 Creating Top Braid Hair

Preparing Geometry for XGen

1) **Separate the Geometry**: Select braidLeft_geo and go to **Mesh > Separate**. This is necessary for applying Tube Groom later in XGen.
2) **Clean Up History**: Select the three separated braid geometries and go to **Edit > Delete by Type > History** to clear any unnecessary history.

Applying XGen Hair

Now that the braid geometry is set up, it's time to apply XGen hair.

Creating a New XGen Description

1) **Create XGen Description**: Select the scalp_geo and go to **XGen > Create Description**.

3. Shaping Each Hair Layer

2) **Set Description Name**: Name the description braidLeft_description (or simply braid_description if you're working on both sides together). Choose **Splines**, set the distribution to **Randomly across the surface**, and enable **Placing and shaping Guides**.

3) Once you create a new description for the braid, you can turn on all Descriptions or switch back and forth between other descriptions, such as the previously created topHair_description, to check how each description is connected. To do this, turn on **Preview All Descriptions in Collection** or switch to other descriptions from the XGen menu (Figure 3.2.5).

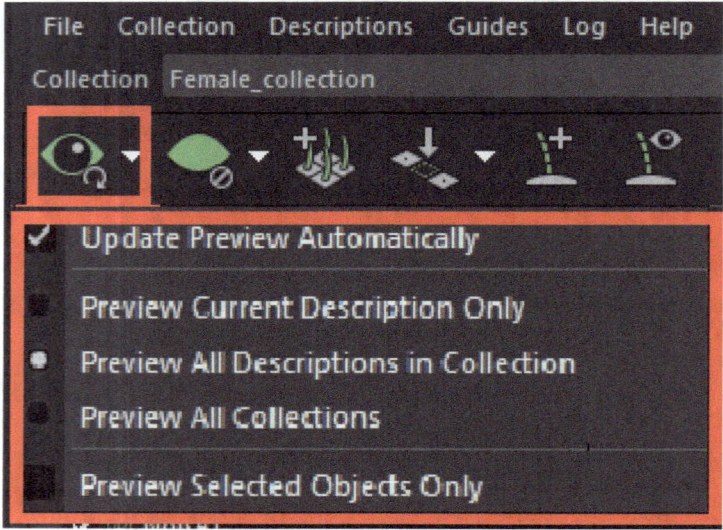

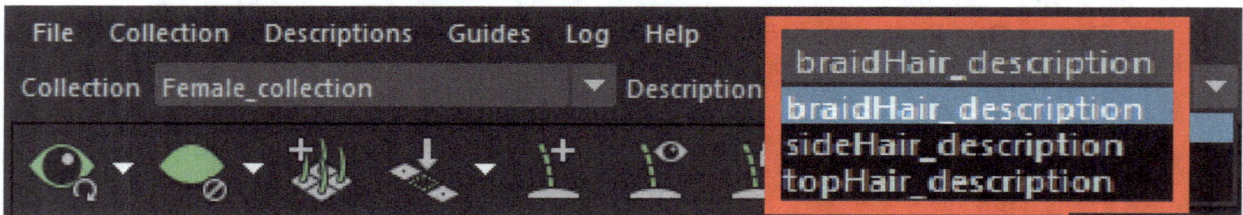

Figure 3.2.5 Selecting description

XGen Essentials: Long Hair Creation with Splines in Maya

Tube Groom Setup

1) **Apply Tube Groom**: Under the **Primitives** tab, expand **Primitive Attributes** and press the **Tube Groom** button.
2) **Assign Tube Geometry**: Select the three left braid geometries and add them to the **Tubes** attribute in the **Tube Based Grooming** window.
3) **Test the Guides**: Press the **Test** button to check if the guides are set. If the guide numbers are still in question marks, troubleshoot by ensuring:

    - ✓ UVs are set to the 0-1 space.
    - ✓ Geometry is properly separated from the three braid parts of the geometry.
    - ✓ Braid polygon geometry have open starts and ends (delete any closed faces).
    - ✓ Faces are arranged correctly.

4) **Adjust Guide Spacing**: Modify the **Guide Spacing** to increase or decrease the number of guides. A setting of 0.5 typically adds more guides.

Creating and Applying a Mask

1) **Create Mask Map**: Under **Generator Attributes**, next to the **Mask** Attribute ▽**Create Map**. Set the resolution to 100 and the start color to Black, then press **Create**.
2) **Paint the Mask**: Using a solid brush, paint the areas where the left side of the braid hair will start, filling them in with white.
3) **Save the Mask**: Once done, press the 💾 **Save** button next to the Mask attribute.

3. Shaping Each Hair Layer

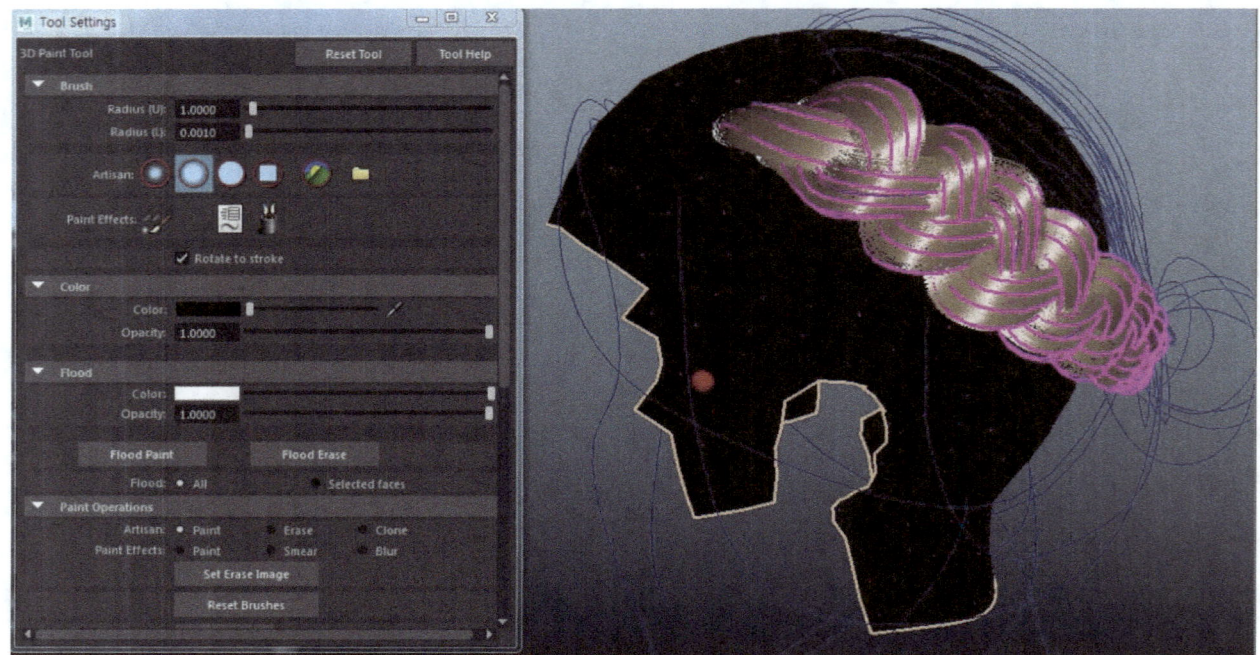

Figure 3.2.6 After Applying the Mask

Refining the Hair

1) **Adjust Density and CV Count**: **Primitives>Generator Attributes** raise the **Density** to around 100-1000, **Primitives>Primitive Attributes** set the **Modifier CV Count** to 50, and adjust the width to create a natural-looking braid.

2) **Sculpt the Guides**: Use the **Sculpt Guides** tool to further refine the shape of the hair.

3) **Add Clumping Modifiers**: Apply a **Clumping** Modifier in the Modifiers tab to add natural clustering to the hair strands.

Creating the Top Braid Hair

After completing the left braid hair, the next step is to create the top section of the braid hair.

Setting Up the Top Hair

1) **Create a New XGen Description**: Start a new XGen description and name it topBraidHair_description.

2) **Match the Guides**: Create guides and adjust them to match the shape of the left braid hair. Figure 3.2.7.

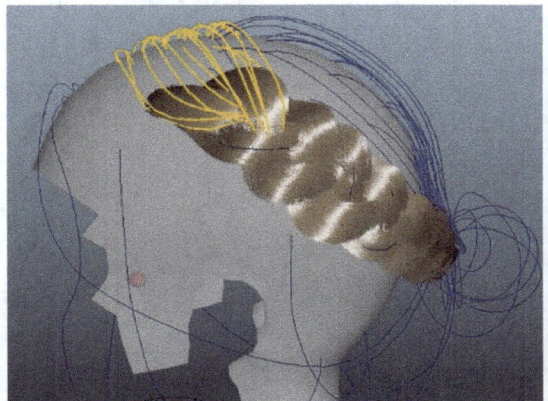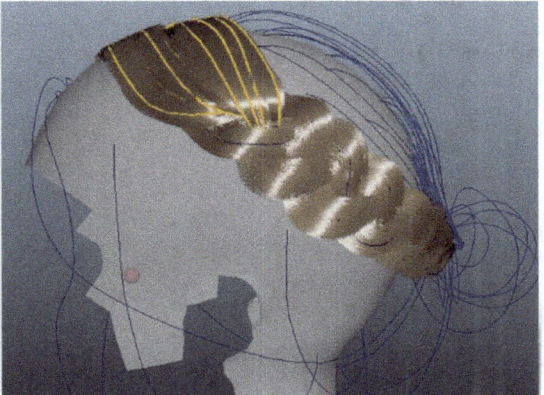

Figure 3.2.7 Matching the Guides

3) **Apply Mask and Adjust Primitives**: Paint mask areas and fine-tune the primitive settings to create a seamless connection with the braid hair.

Creating Braid Hair with Paint Effects

Another method to create braid hair is by using **Paint Effects**. This section explores an alternative approach that uses Maya's Paint Effects to generate braid hair. I will demonstrate how to create the right side using Paint Effects, but you can simply skip this section and mirror the guide curves or duplicate the existing braid geometry to the right side from what we just did.

Creating Curves for Paint Effects

3. Shaping Each Hair Layer

1) **Create Right-Side Braid Curves**: Begin by creating another braid for the right side.
2) **Use Paint Effects**: Although it's not necessary to use Paint Effects, this method will demonstrate another way to create braid hair.
3) **Create the Curve**: Use **Create > Curve Tools > EP Curve Tool** to create a curve from (0,0,0) to (0,40,0).
4) **Switch to FX Mode**: Change the status line to **FX** mode and select **nHair > Make Selected Curves Dynamic**. In the options, set the output to **Paint Effects** and press **Apply**.

Configuring the Paint Effects Braid

1) **Enable Braid Mode**: Select the follicle (child of hairSystem1Follicles), and under **follicleShape** attributes, enable **Braid**.
2) **Adjust Hair System**: Select hairSystem1, and expand the **Clump and Hair Shape**, set **Hairs Per Clump** to 3, **Sub Segments** to 10, and **Clump Width** to 1.4.
3) **Convert to Polygons**: Select pfxHair1 and convert it to polygons by going to **Modify > Convert > Paint Effects to Polygons**.
4) **Smooth the Geometry**: Select the newly created braid geometry and apply **Mesh > Smooth** to refine the shape.
5) **Fine-Tune the Hair**: Go back to the hairSystem shape tab and adjust the **Hair Width** and other settings until the braid hair looks natural. The exact settings will vary depending on your desired style.

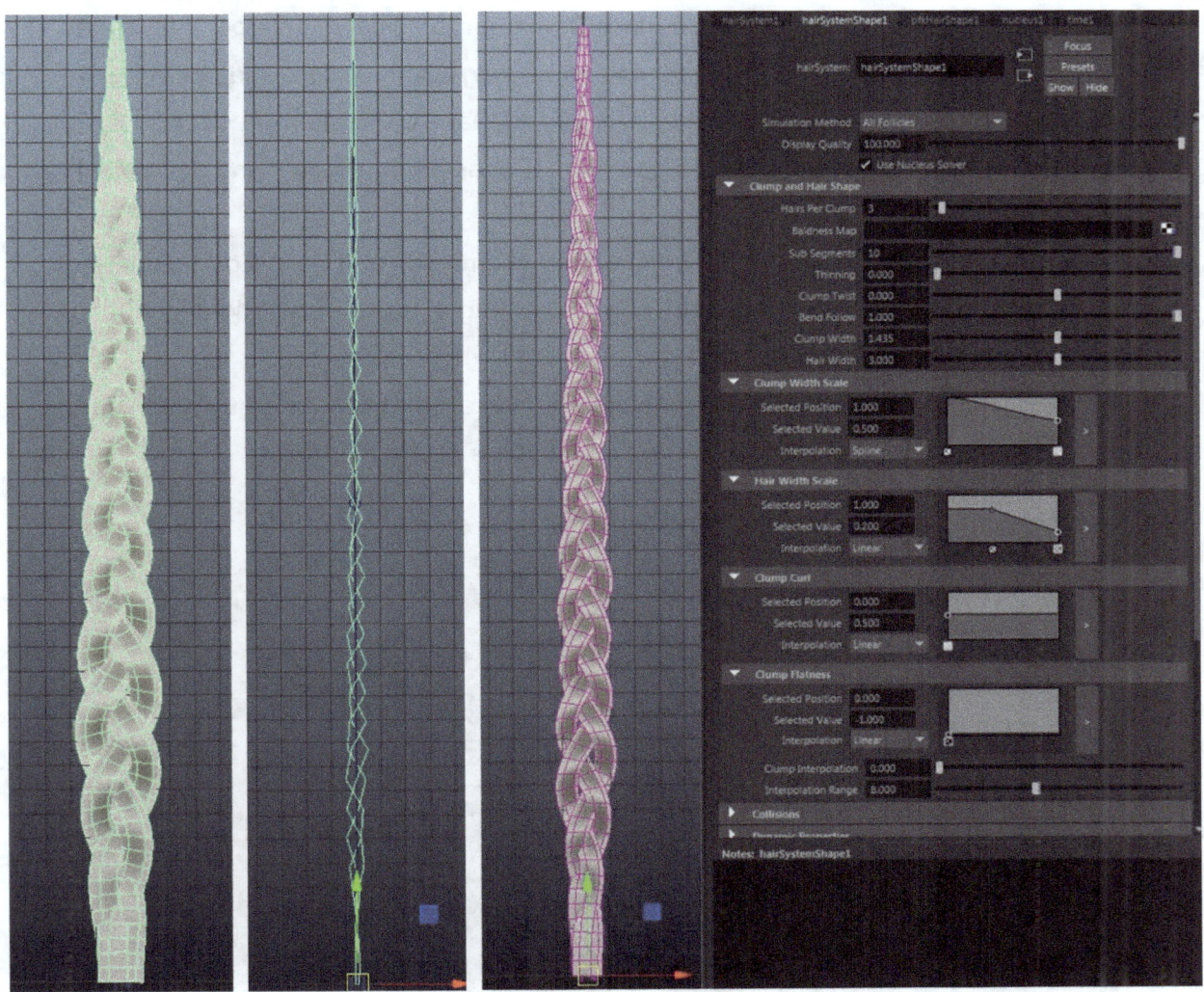

Figure 3.2.8 HairSystem Paint Effects

Finalizing the Right Braid Hair

1) **Clean Up the Scene**: After finalizing the shape of the braid, delete hairSystem1, nucleus1, pfxHair1, and hairSystem1Follicles. Rename the geometry to braidRightDeform_geo.

2) **Shape the Geometry**: Refine the geometry by cutting off unnecessary faces at the top and bottom. Apply **Edit > Delete by Type > History** before starting the deformation process.

3) **Add Deformers and Joints**: Add a **Flare Deformer** to adjust the shape, then create joints as what we did in "Creating Joints and Binding Skin" section, and position the braid on the right side of the scalp. Rotate the joints to shape the braid as needed.
4) **Separate the Geometry**: Once the geometry is shaped, duplicate it and go to **Mesh > Separate**.
5) **Clean Up History**: Select the three right braid geometries and go to **Edit > Delete by Type > History**. Rename each geometry to braidRight_geo01, braidRight_geo02, and braidRight_geo03.
6) **Hide or Delete Unnecessary Geometry**: You can either delete or group and hide the braidRightDeform_geo in case you need to create a new shape later.

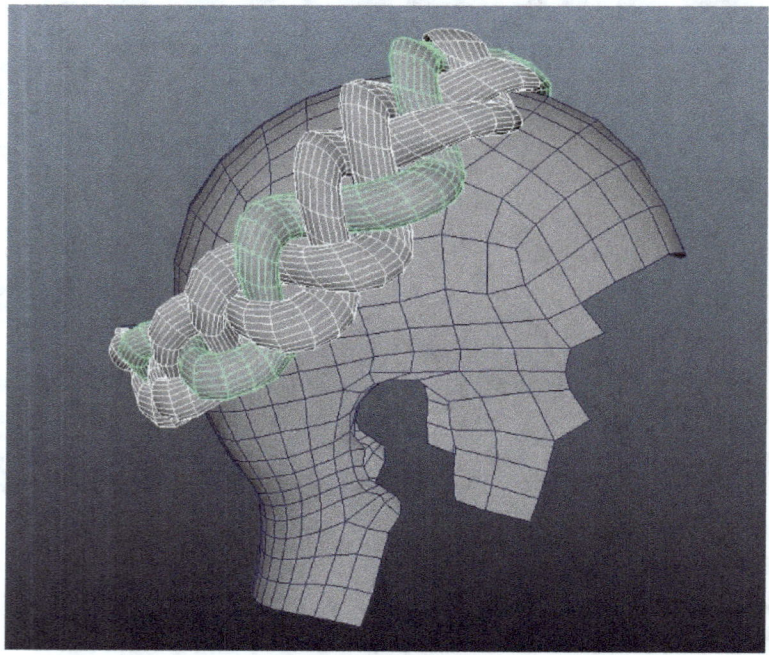

Figure 3.2.9 Finalizing the Right Braid Geometry

Applying XGen Hair to the Right Braid

Follow the same process as described for the left braid to apply XGen hair to the right braid.

1) **Create a New Description**: If needed, select the scalp_geo and create a new description called braidRight_description.

2) **Apply Tube Groom**: Generate guide curves by applying **Tube Groom**, then paint the mask and adjust the CV count and thickness settings. If you're unsure how to do this, go back and review the "Tube Groom Setup."
3) **Add Clumping Modifiers**: Finally, add clumping modifiers to refine the braid hair, ensuring both sides are consistent in appearance.
4) By following these steps, you'll be able to create a realistic and detailed braid hairstyle using XGen, with the option to use Paint Effects for additional variations.

Figure 3.2.10 Finalizing the Right Braid Hair

3.3 Creating Side Hair

In this section, we'll explore how to create side hair using XGen, focusing on creating guide curves, applying masks, and mirroring guides for a balanced hairstyle.

Creating Guide Curves

1) **Create a New XGen Description**

   Select the scalp_geo object and **Create a new XGen Description**. Name the new description sideHair_description.

2) **Select Side Curves**

   Choose the two side curves created in chapter 2.3 that will define the overall shape of the side hair.

3) **Convert Curves to Guides**

   Under the **Utilities** tab, select **Curves to Guides**. Uncheck the **Delete Curves** option and click the **Add Guides** button to generate guide curves from your selected side curves.

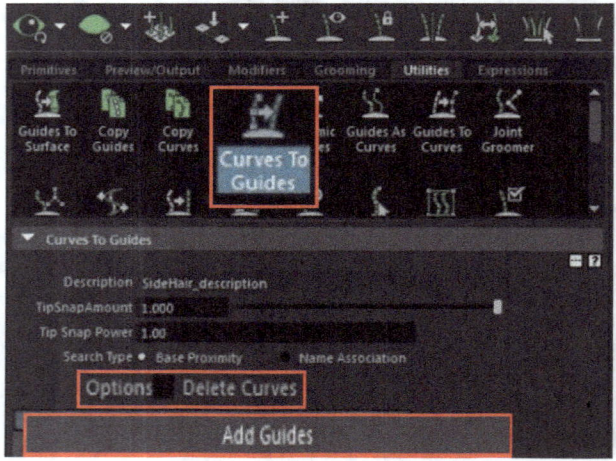 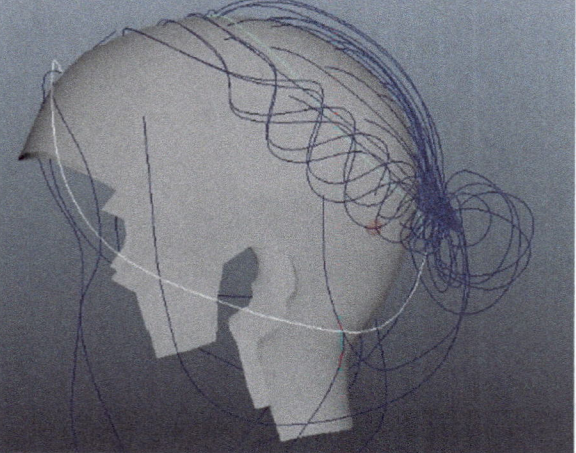

Figure 3.3.1 Convert Curves To Guides

4) **Add Additional Guide Curves**

Insert more guide curves between the existing ones to increase control over the shape of the side hair.

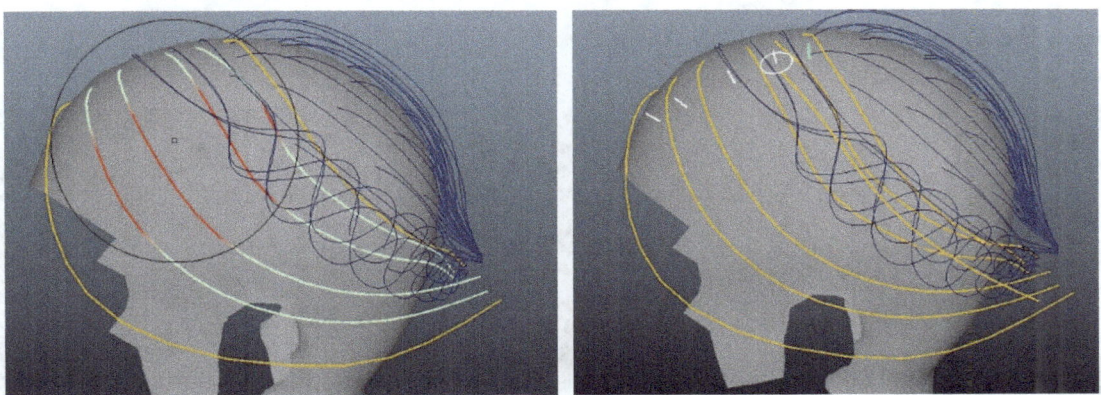

Figure 3.3.2 Adding Additional Guide Curves

5) **Use Copy/Paste Guide Shape**

To work more efficiently, use the **Copy/Paste Guide Shape** feature. This allows you to replicate guide shapes easily and maintain consistency in your hair design.

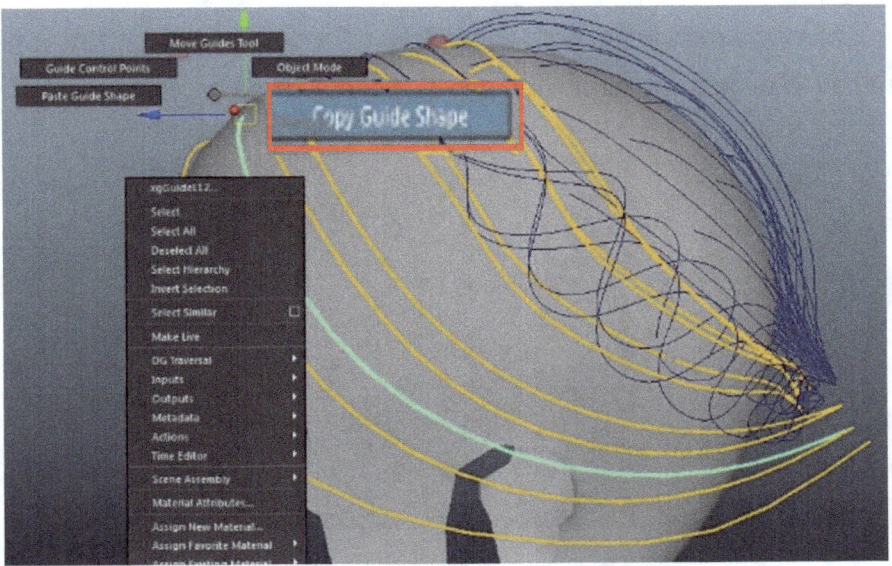

Figure 3.3.3 Copy/Paste Guide Shape

3. Shaping Each Hair Layer

6) **Utilize the Target Guide Tool**:

   To ensure uniformity in your guide shapes, use the **Target Guide** tool under the **Utilities** tab. First, select the guide you want to use as a reference, then click **Set Target**. Next, select other guides and press **Move Selected Guides** to align them with the target guide.

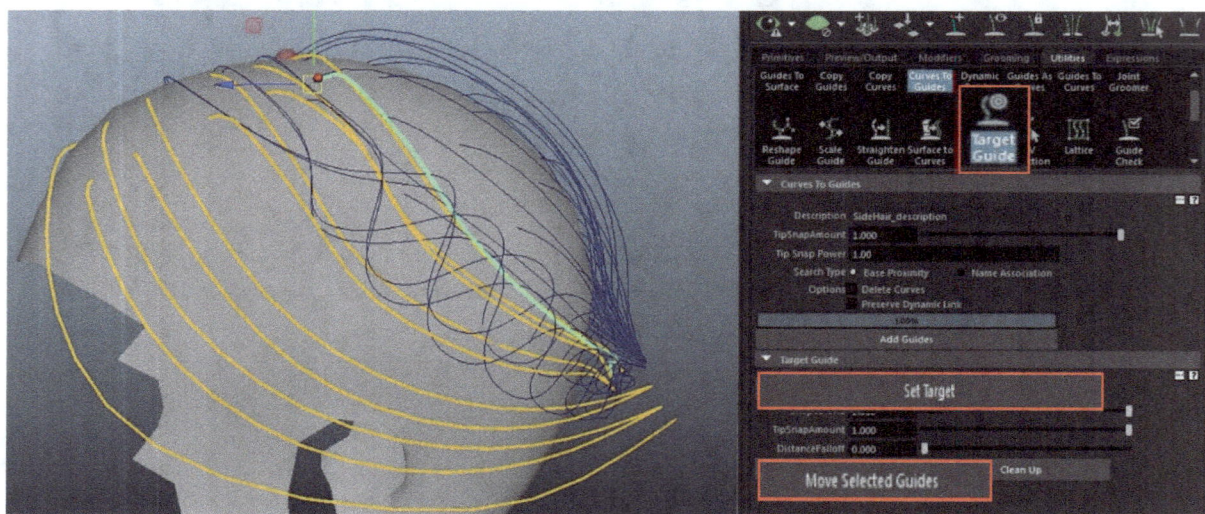

Figure 3.3.4 Target Guide Tool

7) **Rebuild and Normalize Guides**

   Simplify your guides by rebuilding them with a lower CV count. Use the **Normalize** button frequently to even out your guides and achieve a smoother look.

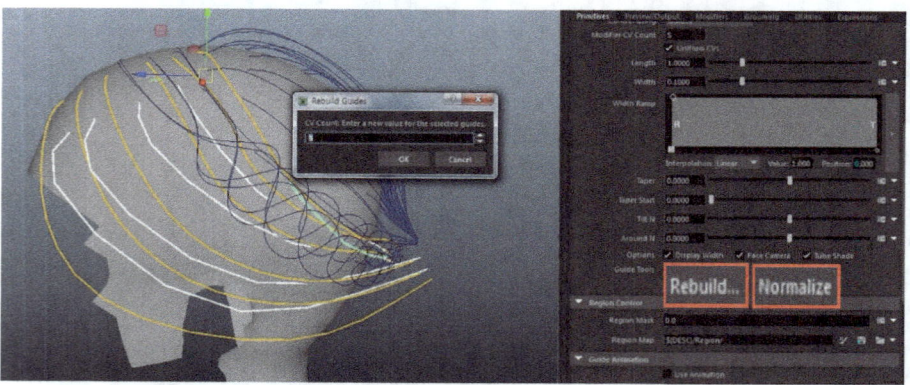

Figure 3.3.5 Rebuiding Guides

Adding a Mask

1) **Create a Mask**

   Once your guides are in place, it's time to mask the regions where the hair will grow. Under the **Primitives** tab, expand the arrow **Mask** attribute and click **Create Map**. Set the map resolution to 100 and the start color to Black, then press **Create**.

2) **Paint the Mask Area**

   Paint the areas where you want the hair to appear using white. After saving the mask, you may notice some primitive hairs appearing under the geometry Figure 3.3.6(right) which can look too bold. Fix this by increasing the **Modifier CV Count** under **Primitive Attributes**—set it to around 30. You may also need to adjust the root shape of your guides to make them stand out more.

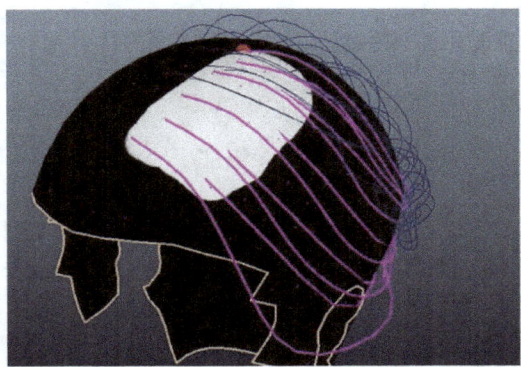 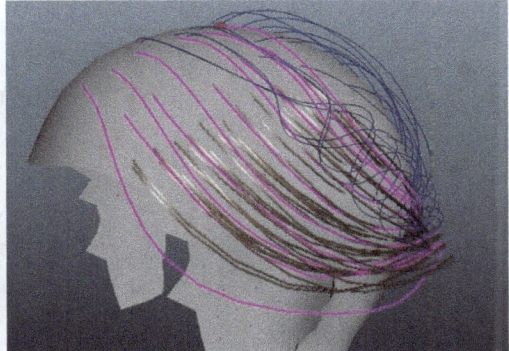

Figure 3.3.6 Paint Mask

3) **Increase Density and Adjust Width**

   Under **Primitives > Generator Attributes**, increase the hair **Density** to over 100. Under **Primitives > Primitive Attributes**, adjust the **Width Ramp** by lowering the root (R circle) and tip (T circle) values in the graph to create a natural tapering effect as shown in Figure 3.3.7.

3. Shaping Each Hair Layer

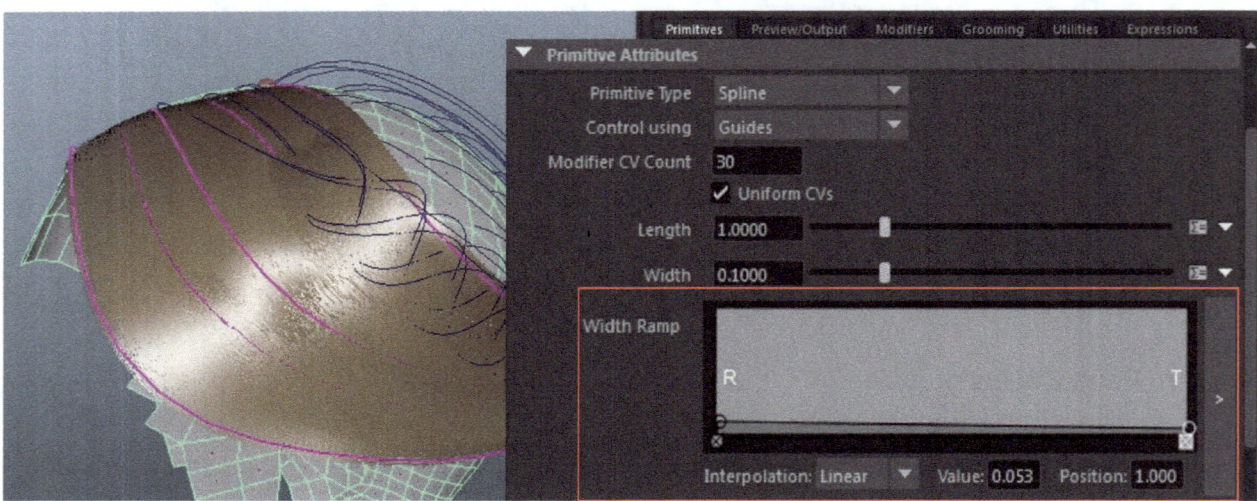

Figure 3.3.7 Adjusting the Width

4) **Mirror the Guides**

   Once you've finished shaping the left side, select the left-side guides and mirror them across the X-axis by pressing the **Mirror Selected Guides Across X-axis** button.

   Figure 3.3.8 XGen Shelf

5) **Reshape for Asymmetry**

   To avoid a symmetrical look, reshape the mirrored guides on the other side to create natural variations.

6) **Set Region Masks and Maps**

Set the **Region Mask** to 1, then create a **Region Map** under **Primitives > Region Control**. Use different colors for the left and right sides, and save the map. For a more natural appearance, consider painting slightly in zigzag patterns.

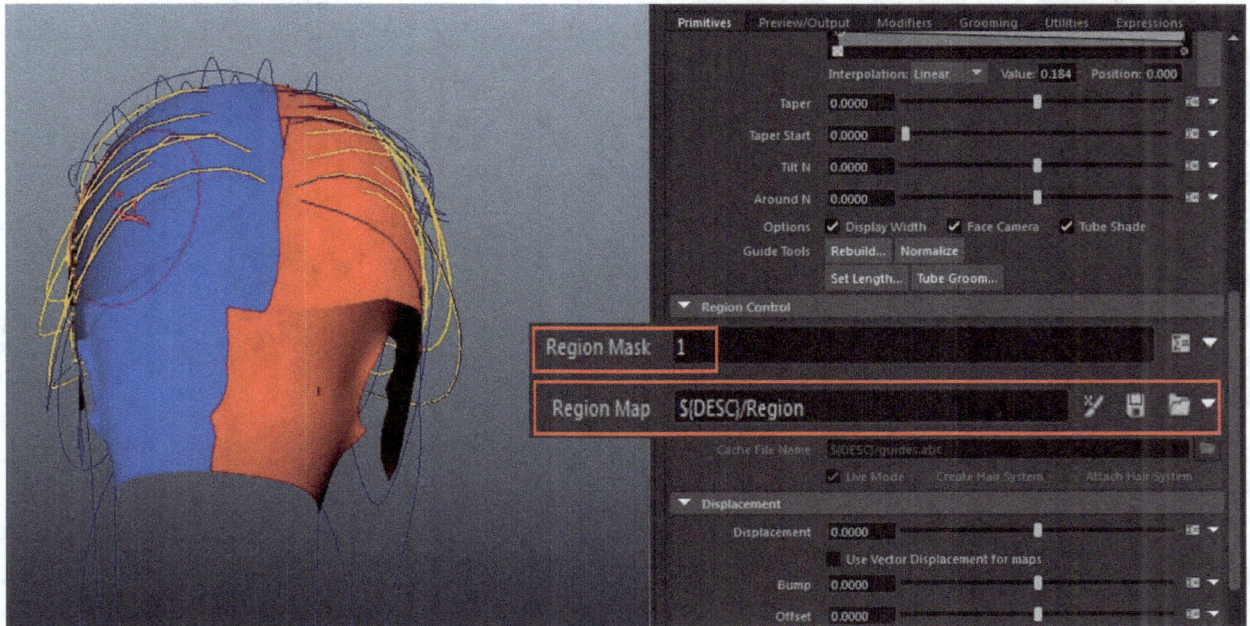

Figure 3.3.9 Set Region Mask

7) **Fine-Tune the Hair Shape**

Adjust the guide curves further to ensure the hair shape fits properly and achieves the desired look.

By following these steps, you will be able to create detailed and natural-looking side hair using XGen.

3. Shaping Each Hair Layer

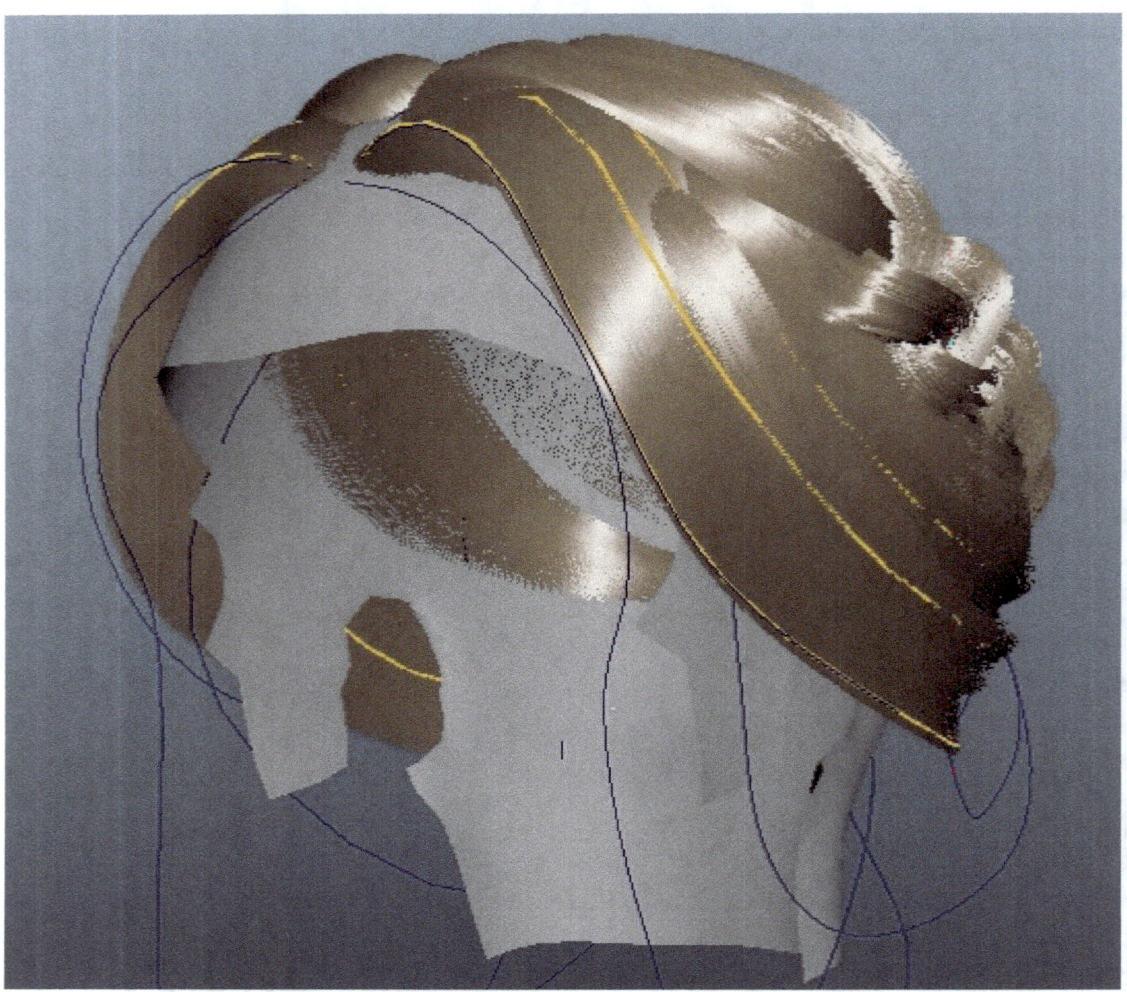

Figure 3.3.10 Side Hair Adjusting Guides

3.4 Creating Low Side Hair

Create Guide Curves

1) Begin by selecting the scalp_geo. Create a new XGen Description, and name it lowSideHair_description.
2) After creating the description, select all the curves that will define the low side hair from chapter 2.3. Navigate to the **Utilities** tab, choose **Curves to Guides**, and click **Add Guides** to convert the curves into guide curves.

3) To enhance the detail, add additional guides between the existing ones. This helps achieve more natural hair flow.

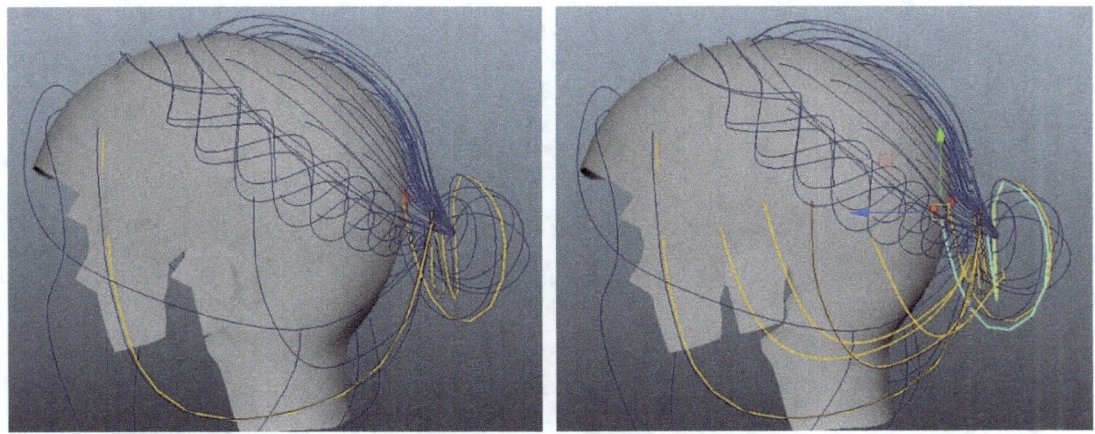

Figure 3.4.1 Create Additional Guides

4) Now, copy the shape of the first guide curve. Paste it onto the in-between guides that were added. An offset will likely appear. To align the new guides, select the first guide as the target, then select all the in-between guides. Use the **Move Selected Guides** option to align them with the first guide.

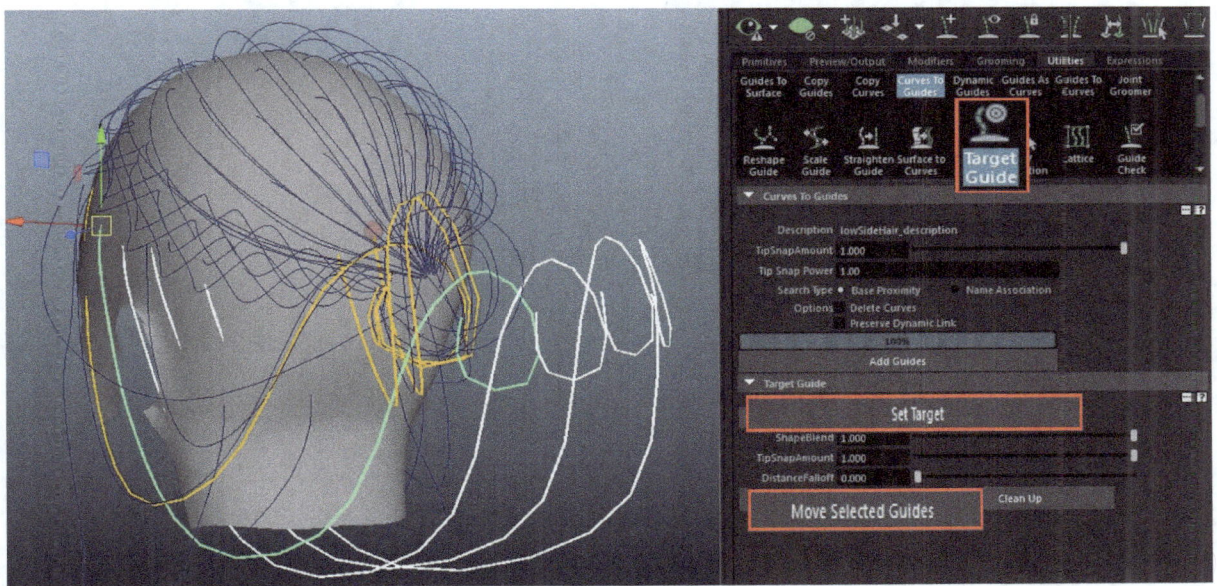

Figure 3.4.2 Move Selected Guides

5) After aligning the guides, manually reshape the in-between guides to refine the overall hair direction and flow.

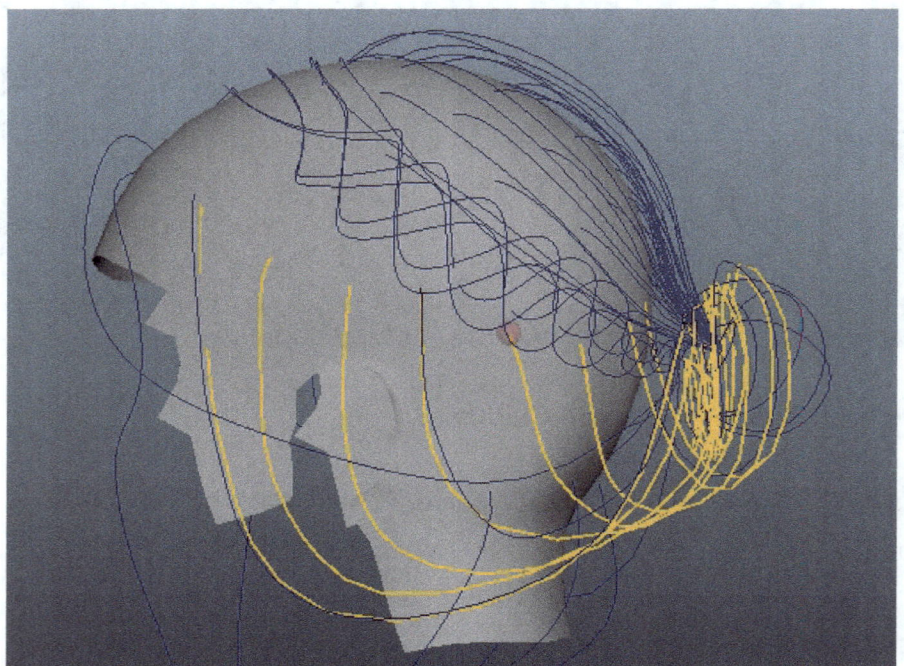

Figure 3.4.3 Reshape In-between Guides

Apply a Mask Map

Once you're satisfied with the guide shapes, switch to the **Primitives** tab. Here, create a **Mask Map**. Use this map to paint the areas on the scalp where you want the hairs to appear. This allows you to control the distribution of hair on the scalp.

XGen Essentials: Long Hair Creation with Splines in Maya

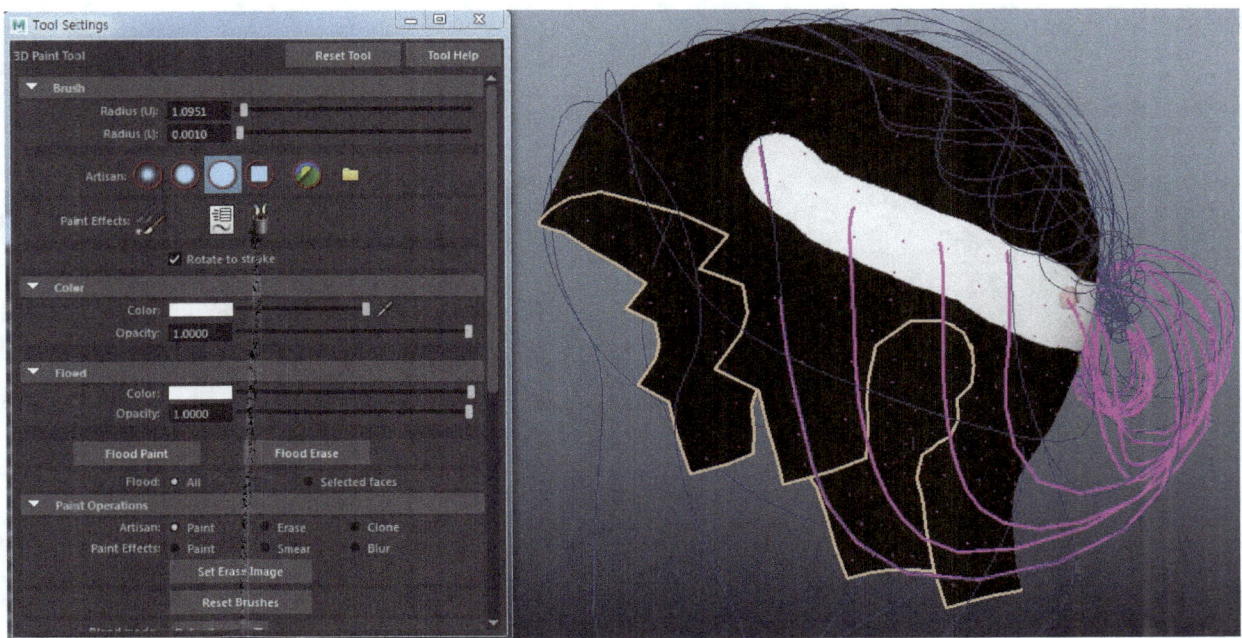

Figure 3.4.4 Apply a Mask Map

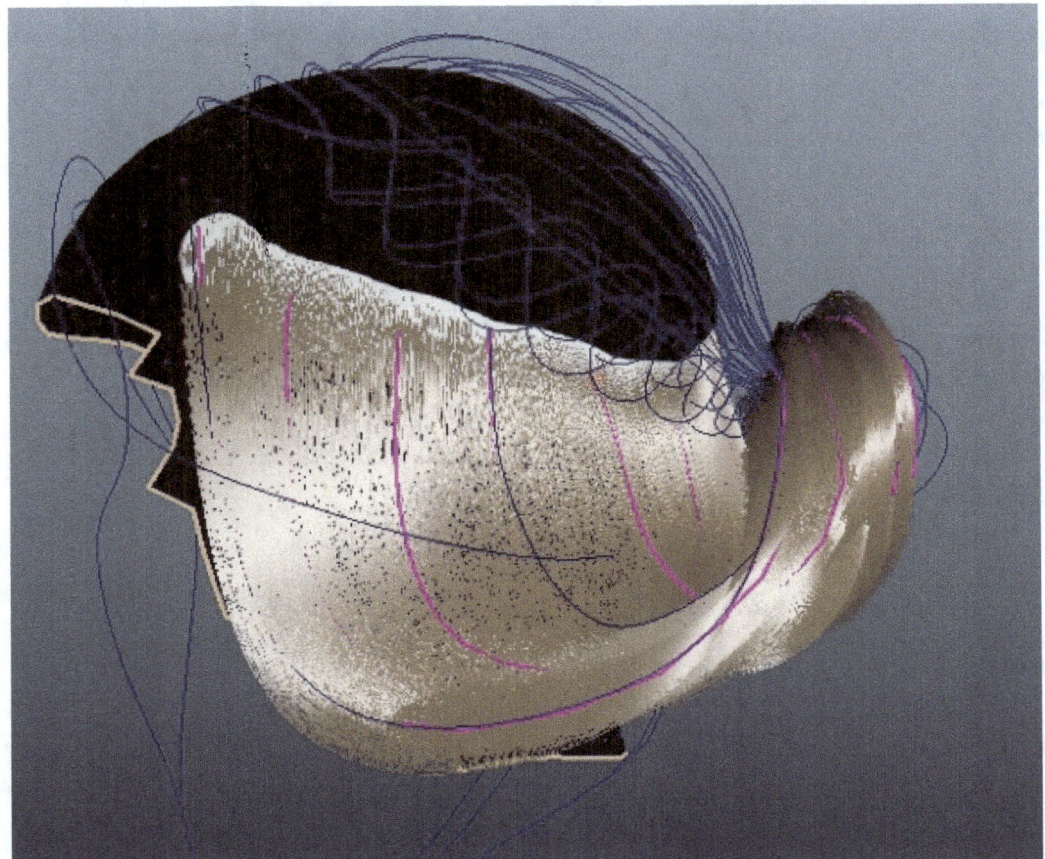

Figure 3.4.5 Hair in the Mask Area

3. Shaping Each Hair Layer

Mirror the Process on the Right Side

Repeat the entire process on the right side of the scalp to ensure asymmetry.

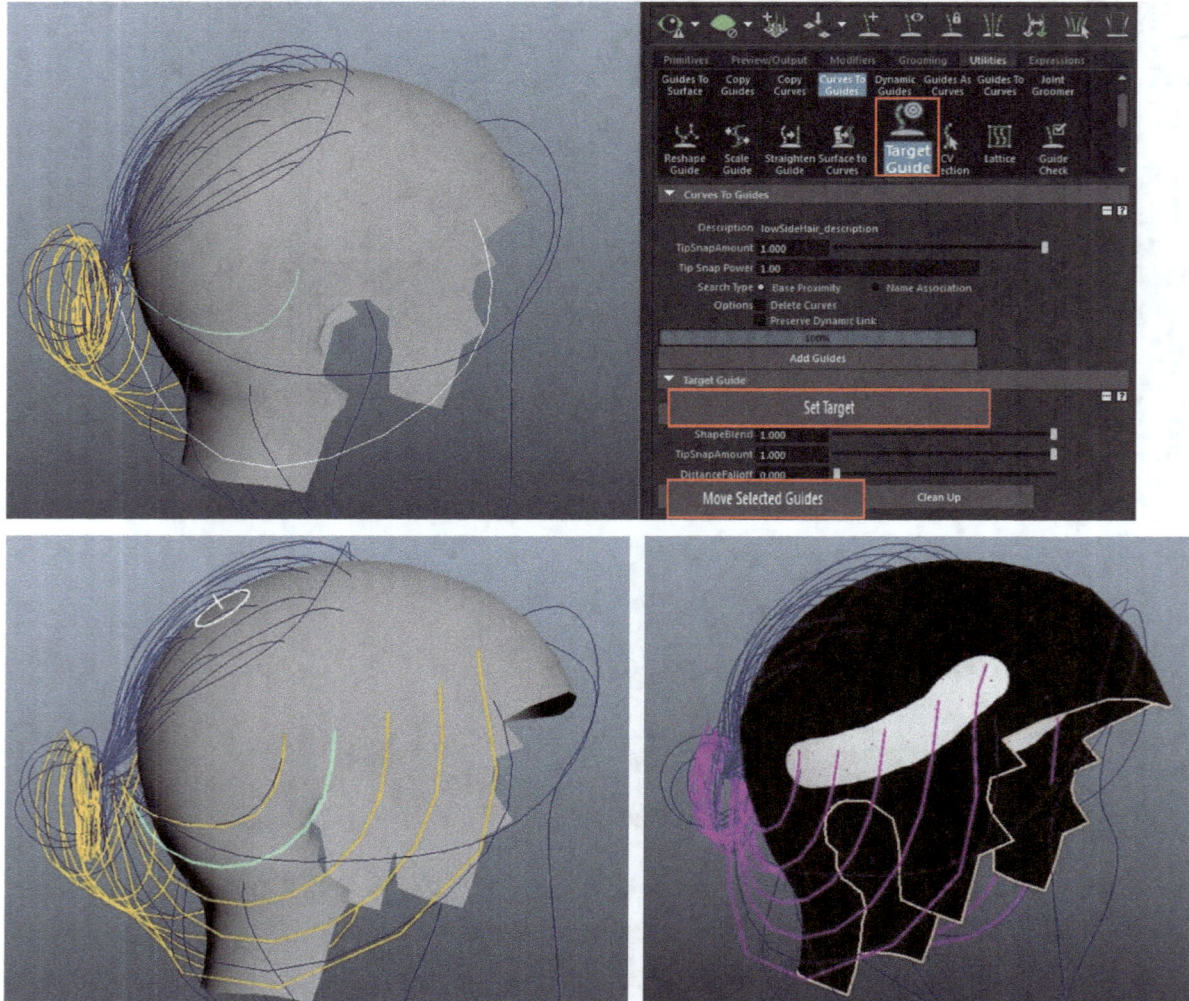

Figure 3.4.6 Right Side Process

Create a Region Map

To differentiate between the left and right sides, create a **Region Map**. This will help you control and separate the two areas more effectively. Be sure to save your work.

XGen Essentials: Long Hair Creation with Splines in Maya

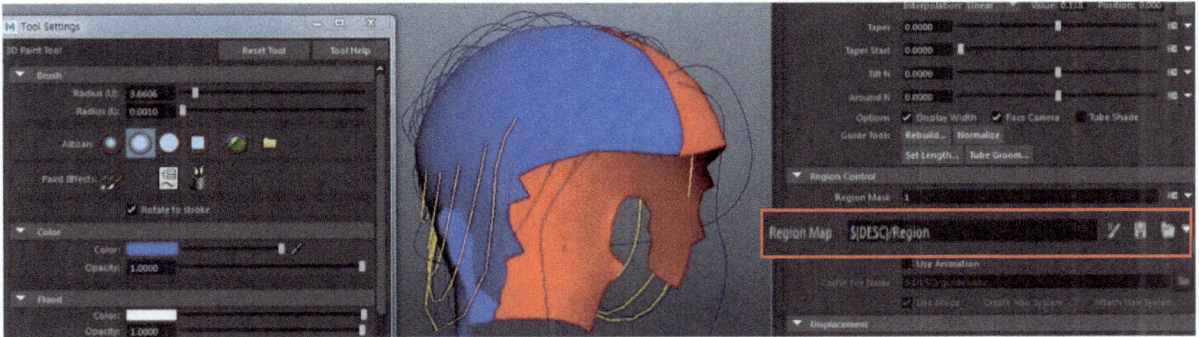

Figure 3.4.7 Region Map

Check the Results

Finally, review the primitive hairs generated by XGen to ensure they match your intended design. Adjustments can be made as needed to achieve the desired appearance.

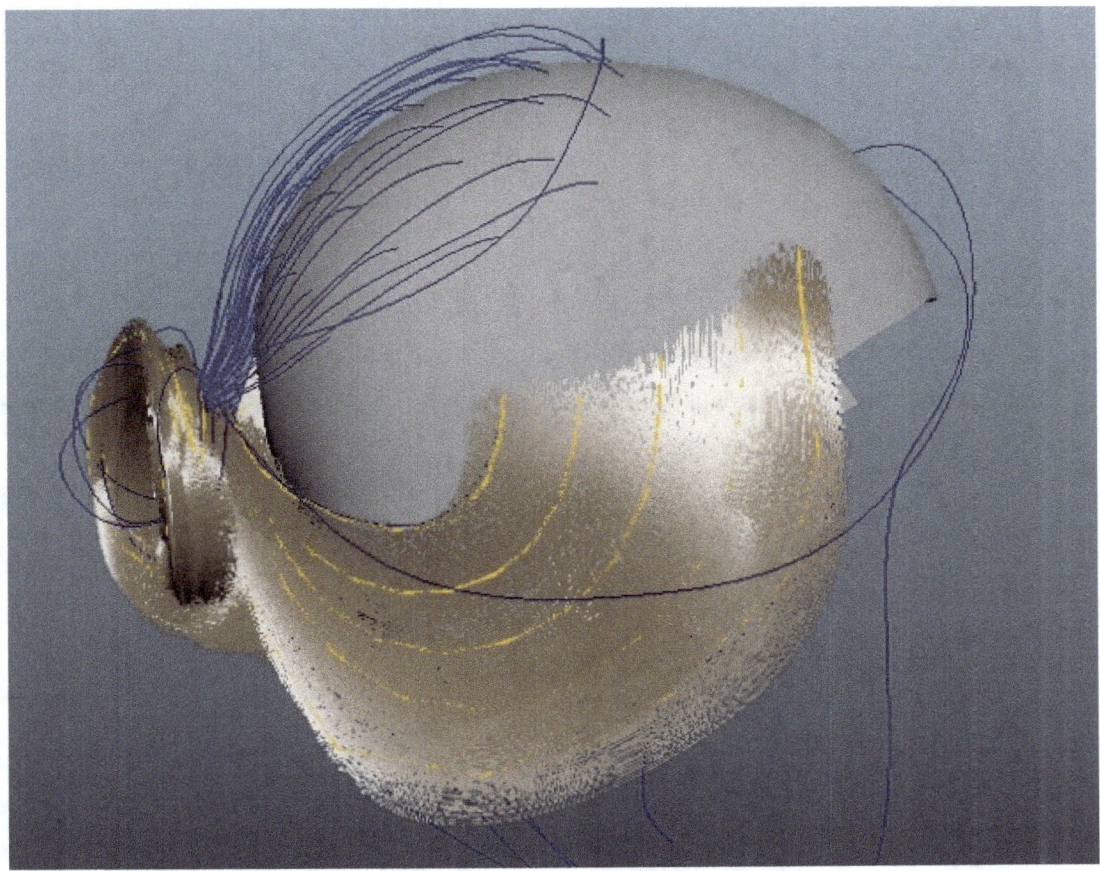

Figure 3.4.8 Low Side Hair Result

3.5 Creating Bangs

In this section, I won't go into as much detail as before, as the process from here on will follow similar steps to what we've already covered. The main difference lies in the specific styling of the bangs. Here's a streamlined guide for creating bangs:

1) **Create a New Description:** Begin by creating a new XGen description for the bangs. Name this description bang_description.
2) **Shape the Hair:** At this point, you have two options: you can shape your hair either by using curves or guides, depending on your preference and the desired outcome.
3) **Create a Mask Map:** Use a mask map to define the areas where the bangs should appear on the scalp. This helps in controlling the hair placement.
4) **Add a Region Map (Optional):** If you need to separate different clumps of hair within the bangs, create and apply a region map to define those areas.
5) **Adjust Hair Properties:** Fine-tune the density and thickness of the hair to match your vision for the bangs.
6) **Add Additional Guide Curves:** If more control is needed, add additional guide curves to refine the shape and direction of the hair.
7) **Use Target Guide:** Under the **Utilities** tab, select **Target Guide** to lump the guide curves together, ensuring they follow the desired direction and flow.
8) **Apply Clump Modifiers:** Finally, add clump modifiers to preview how the bangs will look when clumped. This will help you see the overall shape and make any necessary adjustments to achieve the desired result.

XGen Essentials: Long Hair Creation with Splines in Maya

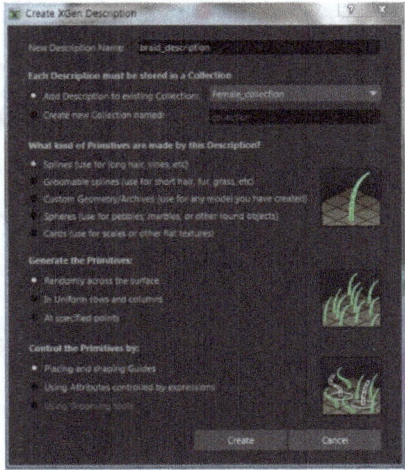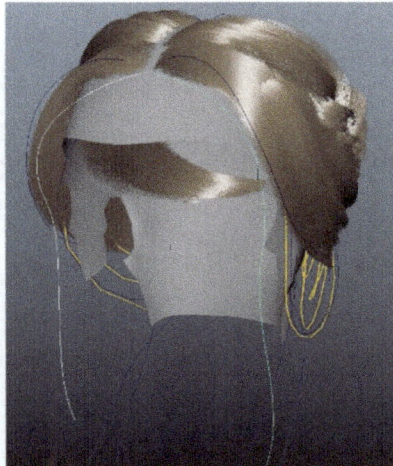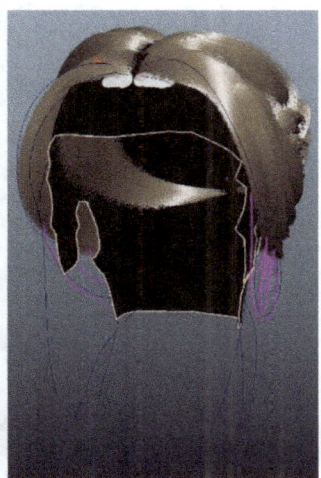
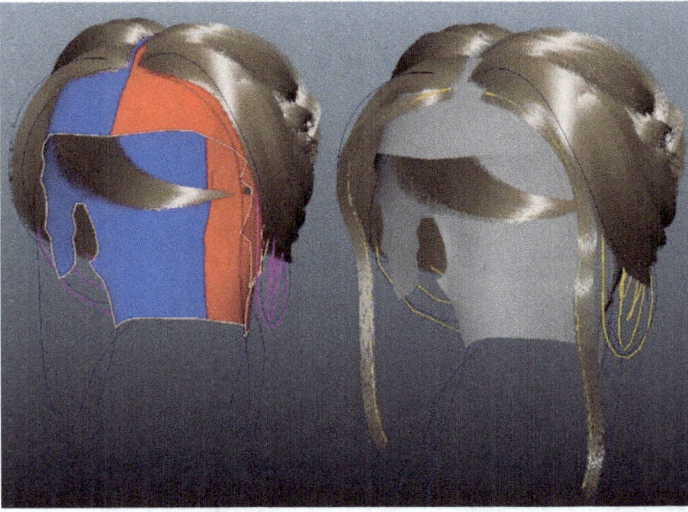

Figure 3.5.1 Bangs Process

3.6 Creating a Bun

1) **Create a New Description:** Start by creating a new XGen description for the bun. Name this description bun_description.
2) **Create and Shape Guides:** Generate guide curves and shape them to form the bun, ensuring they cover the tied-up area at the back of the head. **Create a Mask Map:** As before, use a mask map to define where the bun hair should appear on the scalp. This allows you to control the hair placement specifically within the bun area.

3) **Add a Region Map (Optional):** If you need to separate the bun into different clumps for more detailed styling, create and apply a region map to manage those sections effectively.

4) **Adjust Hair Properties:** Fine-tune the hair density and thickness to achieve the right volume and texture for the bun.

5) **Add Additional Guide Curves:** If more control is needed to perfect the bun's shape, add additional guide curves as necessary.

6) **Apply Clump Modifiers:** Lastly, apply clump modifiers to see how the hair will look when clumped together. This will give you a better sense of the overall shape and form of the bun, allowing for final adjustments to achieve the desired style.

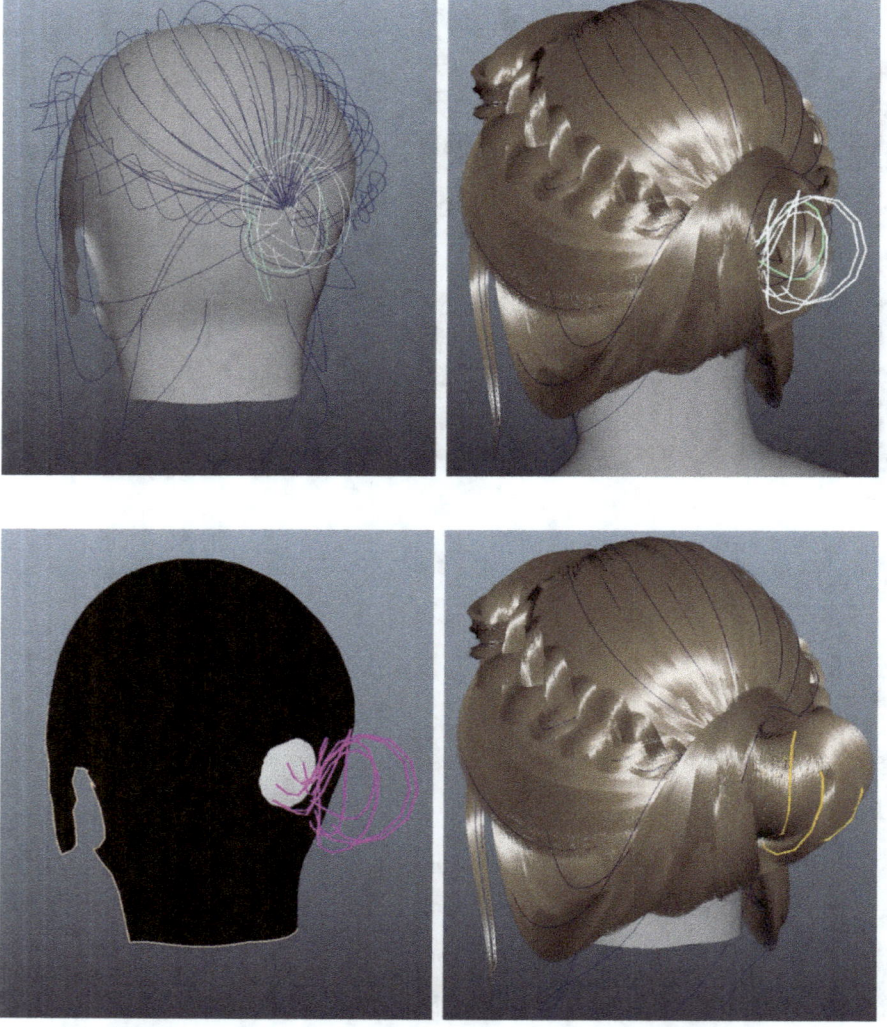

Figure 3.6.1 Bun Hairstyle Process

3.7 Creating Long Hair (Left, Right, and Back)

1) **Create a New Description:** Start by creating a new XGen description for the long hair. Name this description longHair_description.
2) **Shape the Hair:** You can shape the long hair using either curves or guides, depending on your preference. To create a fuller, more voluminous look, you may need to add additional guides throughout the hair.
3) **Create a Mask Map:** Use a mask map to control where the long hair appears on the scalp, ensuring the hair only grows in the desired areas.
4) **Add a Region Map:** To effectively manage the long hair, create a region map to separate the left and right sections. This will help with more precise control over the styling of each side.
5) **Adjust Hair Properties:** Adjust the density and thickness of the hair to achieve the look and feel you're aiming for. This step is essential for making the long hair appear natural and well-integrated.
6) **Add Additional Guides:** If necessary, continue to add more guide curves to refine the shape and flow of the long hair.
7) **Apply Clump Modifiers:** Once your guides are in place, apply clump modifiers to preview how the hair will look when clumped together. This will give you a sense of the final styling and volume.
8) **Clump Modifier Considerations:** If you add more guides after setting up the clump modifiers, be aware that the clumping may not update correctly. In this case, you will need to reset and configure the clump maps again to ensure they work properly with the new guides.

3. Shaping Each Hair Layer

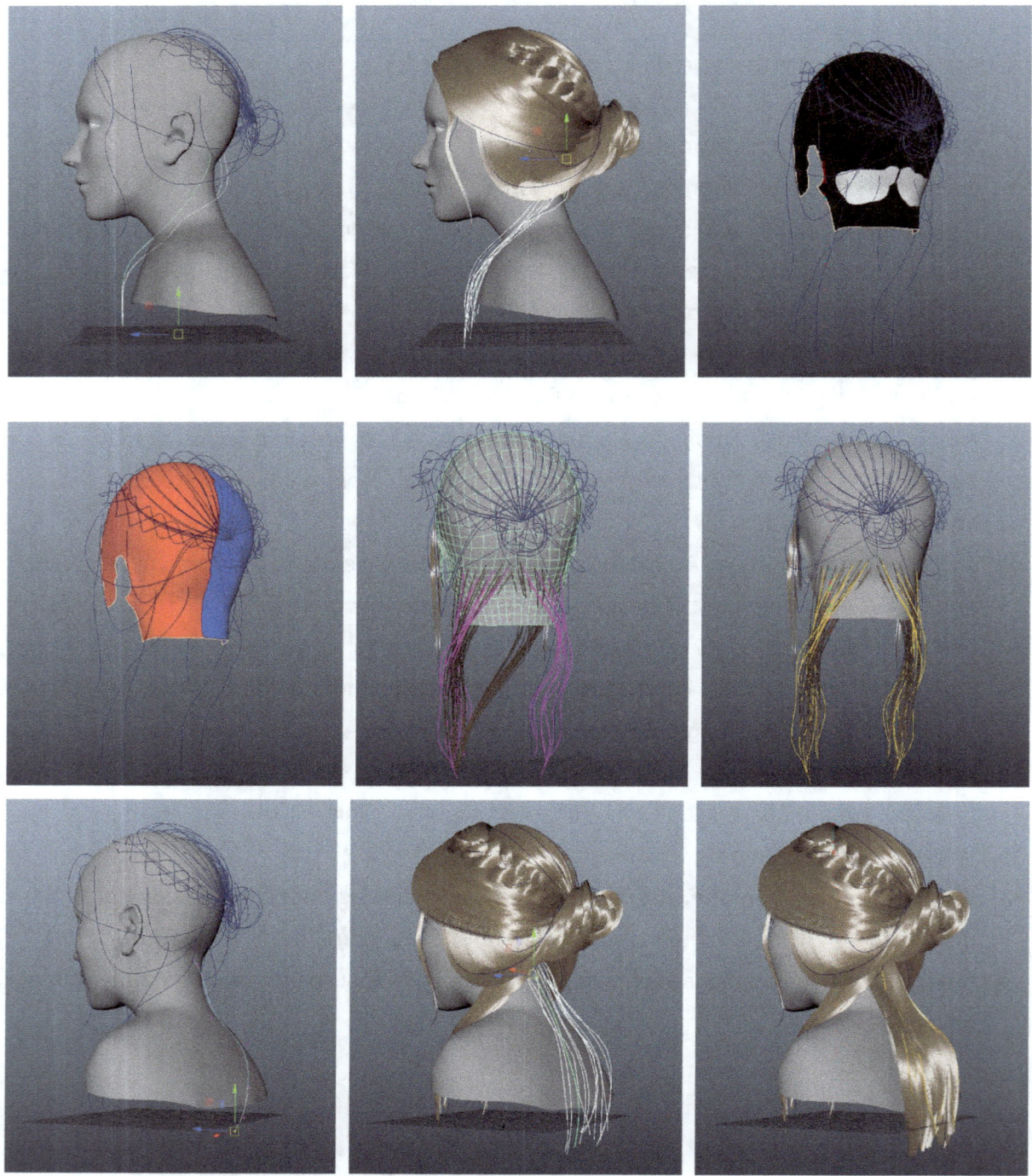

Figure 3.7.1 Creating Long Hair Process

3.8 Creating Sideburns (Left and Right)

1) **Create a New Description:** Start by creating a new XGen description specifically for the sideburns. Name this description sideburn_description.
2) **Shape the Hair:** You can shape the sideburns using either curves or guides, depending on your workflow. Focus on achieving the correct length and direction for the sideburns to blend naturally with the rest of the hairstyle.
3) **Create a Mask Map:** Use a mask map to specify where the sideburns should appear on the scalp, allowing precise control over their placement.
4) **Add a Region Map:** To manage the left and right sideburns independently, create a region map. This will help you separate and control each side for more detailed styling.
5) **Adjust Hair Properties:** Fine-tune the density and thickness of the sideburn hair to ensure it looks natural and proportional compared to the other parts of the hair.
6) **Add Additional Guides:** If more control is required to refine the sideburns, add additional guide curves as needed to adjust their shape and flow.
7) **Apply Clump Modifiers:** Apply clump modifiers to see how the sideburns will look when clumped. This helps in achieving a more realistic appearance, particularly with the fine hairs that make up sideburns.
8) **Check the Overall Look:** Once you've completed the sideburns, check how they integrate with the rest of the hair. Make any necessary adjustments to ensure the sideburns blend seamlessly with the overall hairstyle.

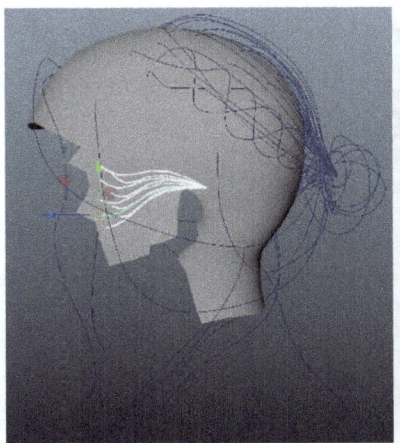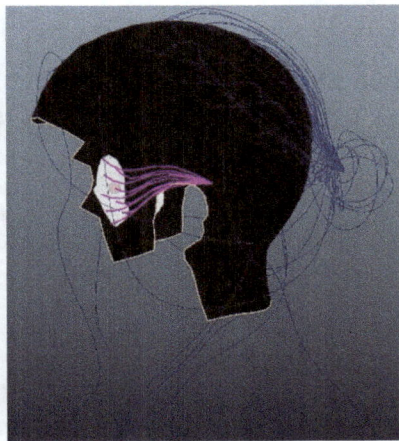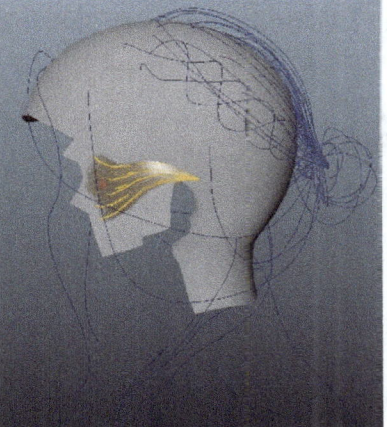

Figure 3.8.1 Steps for Creating Sideburns

3.9 Creating Messy Hair at the Back

1) **Create a New Description:** Start by creating a new XGen description for the messy hair at the back. Name this description messyHairBack_description.

2) **Shape the Hair:** Shape the messy hair using either curves or guides. Since the messy hair originates from the bun at the back, it may be helpful to copy one of the existing bun curves and reshape it to create a messy hair look. Once you've shaped the initial guide, add more guides around it to create a fuller, more natural look. Be mindful not to position the guides at the same starting point, as this can cause issues with guide clumping and hair primitive generation.

3) **Create a Mask Map:** Use a mask map to define where the messy hair should appear on the scalp. This helps control the placement and ensures the hair grows only in the desired areas.

4) **Adjust Hair Properties:** Adjust the density and thickness of the messy hair to match the intended look. Messy hair often has varying density, so be sure to balance these settings for a realistic appearance.

5) **Add Additional Guides:** If necessary, add more guide curves to refine the overall shape and volume of the messy hair.

6) **Apply Clump Modifiers:** Once the guides are set, apply clump modifiers to see how the hair looks when clumped together. This will give the messy hair its characteristic texture and flow.

7) **Check the Overall Look:** Finally, review the messy hair in conjunction with the rest of the hairstyle. Make sure it integrates seamlessly with the bun at the back and the other hair sections, adjusting as needed to achieve a cohesive look.

XGen Essentials: Long Hair Creation with Splines in Maya

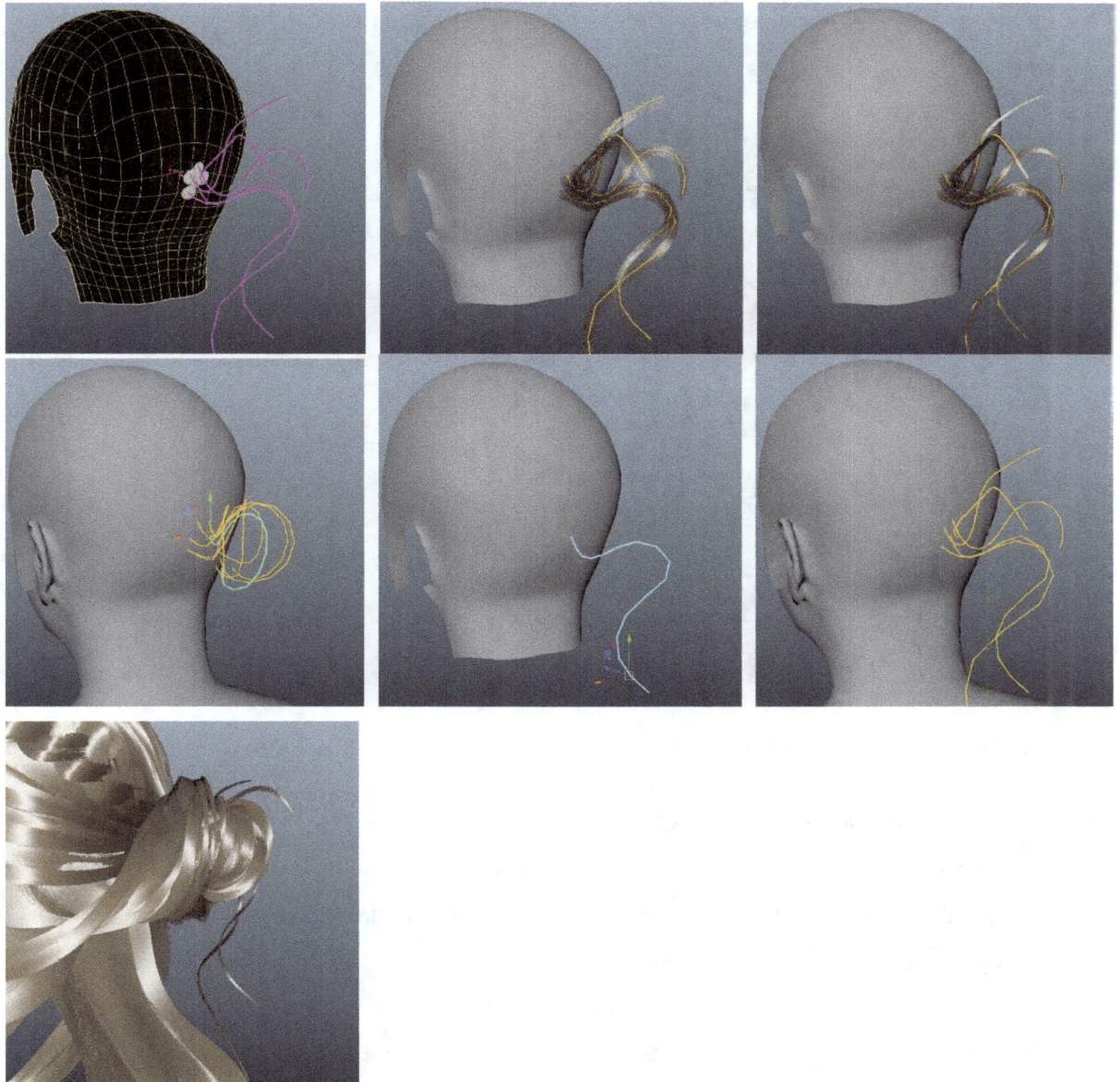

Figure 3.9.1 Process for Creating Messy Hair Back

3.10 Creating Flyaway Hair

1) **Create a New Description:** Begin by creating a new XGen description specifically for the flyaway hairs. Name this description flyaway_description.
2) **Shape the Hair:** Shape the flyaway hairs using either curves or guides. To ensure the flyaway hairs blend naturally with the rest of the hairstyle, it may be helpful to visualize

other parts of the primitive hairs to determine the appropriate placement for the flyaway strands.

Figure 3.10.1 Creating Flyaway Hair

3) **Create a Mask Map:** Use a mask map to define the areas where the flyaway hairs should appear. For more control over the distribution, consider using different artisan brushes in the **3D Paint Tool** window. By clicking the folder icon, you can select a variety of brushes. For flyaway hairs, a spotty brush shape (available in Maya) often works well for a more random distribution. Alternatively, you can create custom brush shapes in Photoshop and load them into Maya to suit your specific needs.

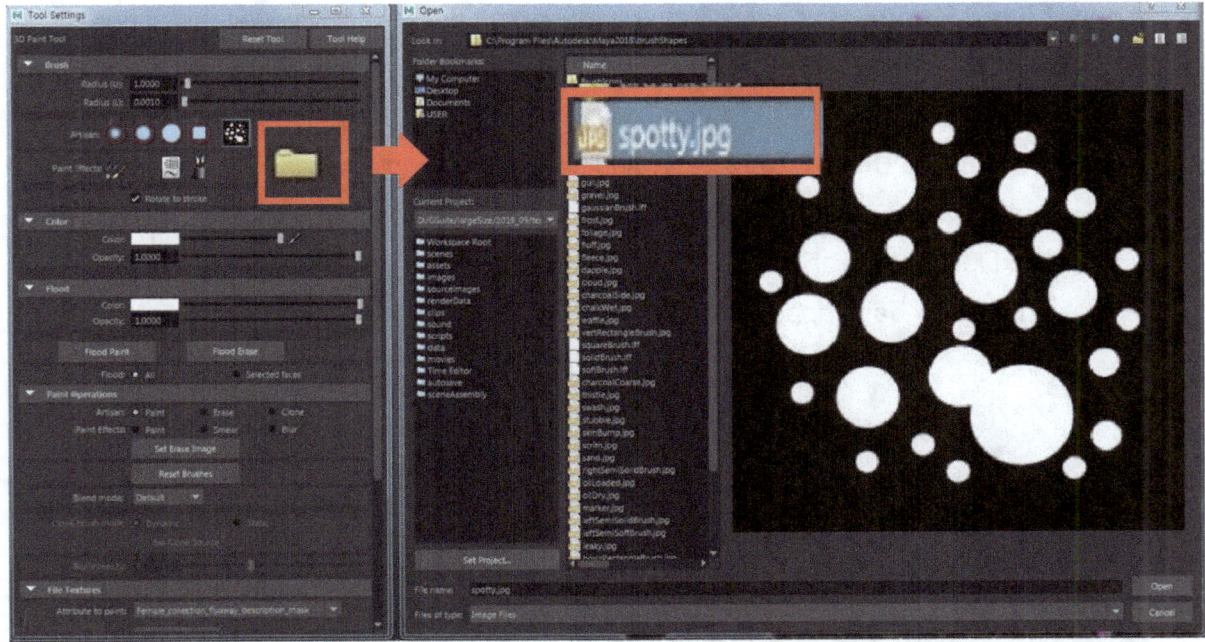

Figure 3.10.2 3D Paint Tool Brush Settings

4) **Adjust Hair Properties:** Adjust the density and thickness of the flyaway hairs. Since flyaway hairs are typically thinner than the rest of the hair, you'll want to reduce the thickness and possibly adjust the density for a more delicate appearance.

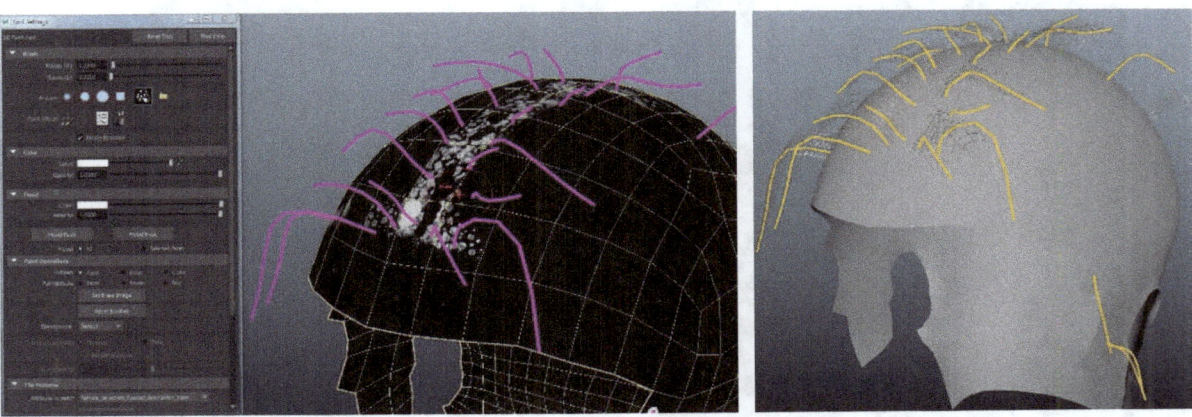

Figure 3.10.3 Painting the Flyaway Hair Area

5) **Add Additional Guides:** If needed, add more guide curves to further refine the look and direction of the flyaway hairs.

6) **Apply Clump Modifiers:** Apply clump modifiers to see how the flyaway hairs behave when clumped together. This step is essential for achieving a more realistic and natural flyaway effect.
7) **Consider Multiple Descriptions:** Depending on the complexity and distribution of the flyaway hairs, you may need to create additional flyaway descriptions for a more refined and layered look. This can help achieve better variation and randomness, which are key to making flyaway hairs appear natural.

Figure 3.10.4 Flyaway Hair

XGen Essentials: Long Hair Creation with Splines in Maya

4. Enhancing Hair with XGen Modifiers

XGen modifiers are powerful tools that enable the creation of realistic and dynamic hair styles with minimal manual adjustments. These modifiers allow you to introduce curls, waves, trimming effects, and even simulate natural hair movements. By leveraging XGen modifiers, you can achieve a variety of hairstyles efficiently while ensuring they appear believable.

When using modifiers, it's essential to follow a structured approach. Typically, it's recommended to begin with clumping, as XGen processes clumping first in the modifier stack. In earlier lessons, we explored the basics of shaping hair and applied simple clumping modifiers to each description. Now, let's delve into the most commonly used modifiers and learn how to refine hair with them.

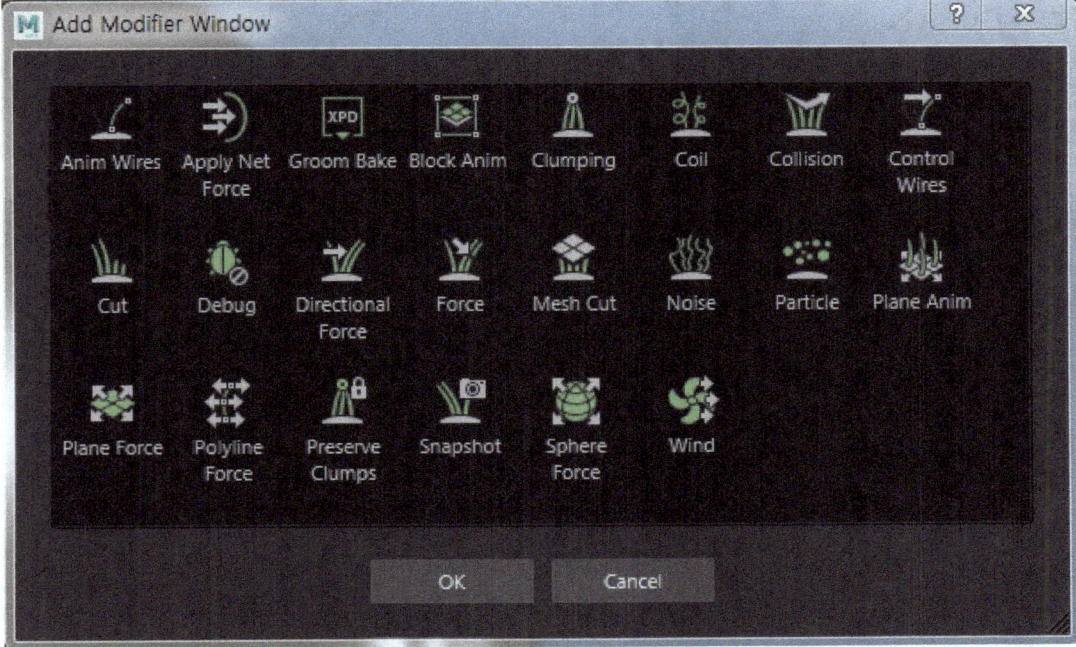

Figure 4 Modifier Window

4. Applying Modifiers in XGen

4.1 Modifiers: Top Hair

We'll start by applying modifiers to the top hair, as this serves as a good foundation. The process will be similar for other hair descriptions, so we'll briefly touch on those later.

Clumping:

It's generally beneficial to use at least two clumping modifiers for each hair description. The first clump groups the hair broadly, while additional clumps refine it into smaller sections.

Whenever new guides are added, you must re-upload the clump modifier to ensure the clumps align correctly with the new guides. To do this, press the **Setup Maps** button in the Clumping Modifiers tab, **Curl Effect** section, then press the **Guide** button to synchronize the clumps with your guides. Alternatively, you can increase the density and press the **Generate** to have more or less clumps depending on the density. Finally, press **Save** to complete the clump.

Under the clumping modifier, enable the color preview to visualize how your clumps are distributed. XGen assigns random colors to each clump, making it easier to see the distinctions.

Figure 4.1.1 Clumping Modifier: Enable Color Preview

For further refinement, adjust the clump scale graph. The left "R" and right "T" circles on the graph represent the root and tip of the hair, respectively. Moving these points up or down alters the clump's shape, allowing you to create concave or convex forms. You can add additional points to the graph for more complex clumping shapes (Figure 4.1.2).

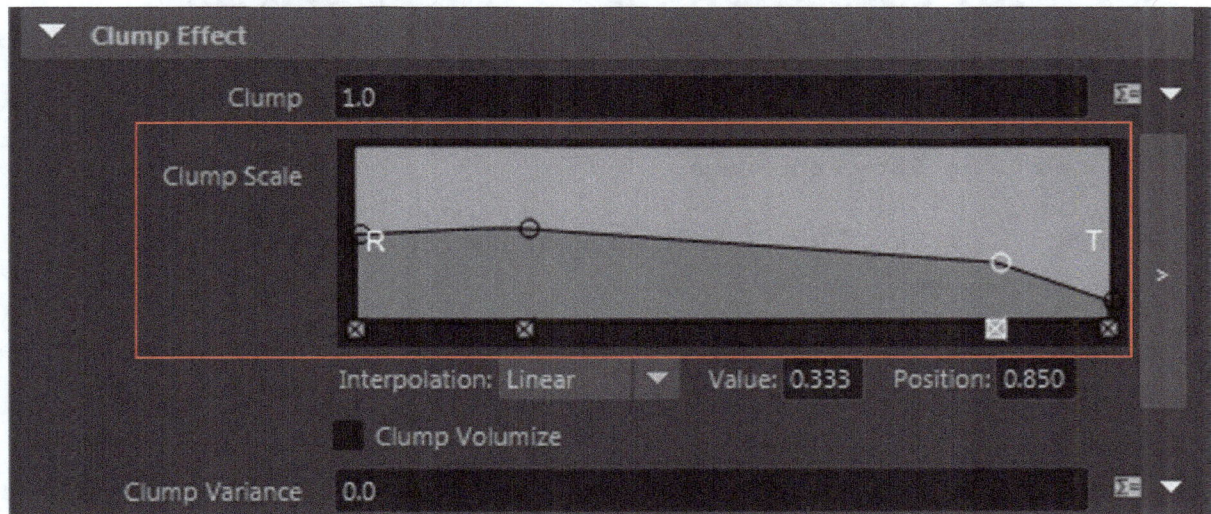

Figure 4.1.2 Clump Scale

Once the clump shape is satisfactory, turn off the color preview and add more clumping modifiers on top if necessary.

Noise:
Next apply the Noise modifier. This modifier introduces curls to the hair. Even for characters with straight hair, it's often useful to add a small amount of noise to simulate stray curls. If you want uniform noise across the entire hair, simply increase the magnitude.

To add stray curly hairs selectively, you can use one of two methods:

- Set a stray percentage from the XGen **Descriptions** menu. Select **Descriptions > Set Stray Percentage** and enter a value (e.g., 10 for 10%). Once set, type stray()?1:0 under the Noise Modifier's Mask or Magnitude attribute to apply the noise to 10% of the hair.

4. Applying Modifiers in XGen

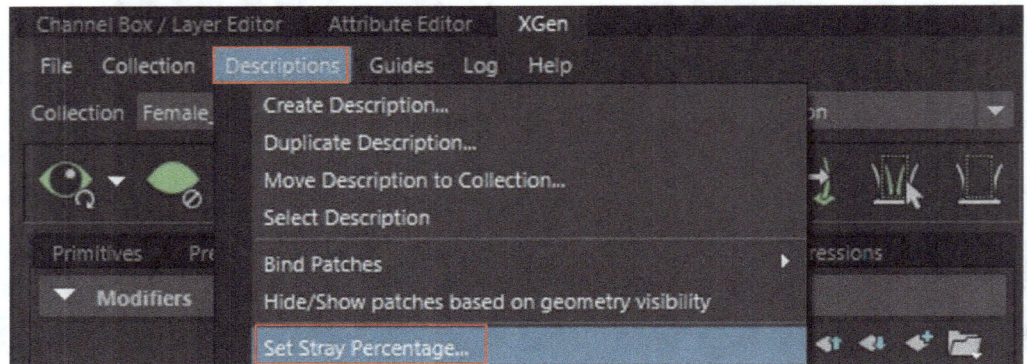

Figure 4.1.3 Set Stray Percentage

- Alternatively, use the expression editor next to the Noise Modifier's Mask attribute. In the expression editor, type:

$percentStray=10.0000; #0.0, 100.0

rand()<$percentStray/100.0?1:0

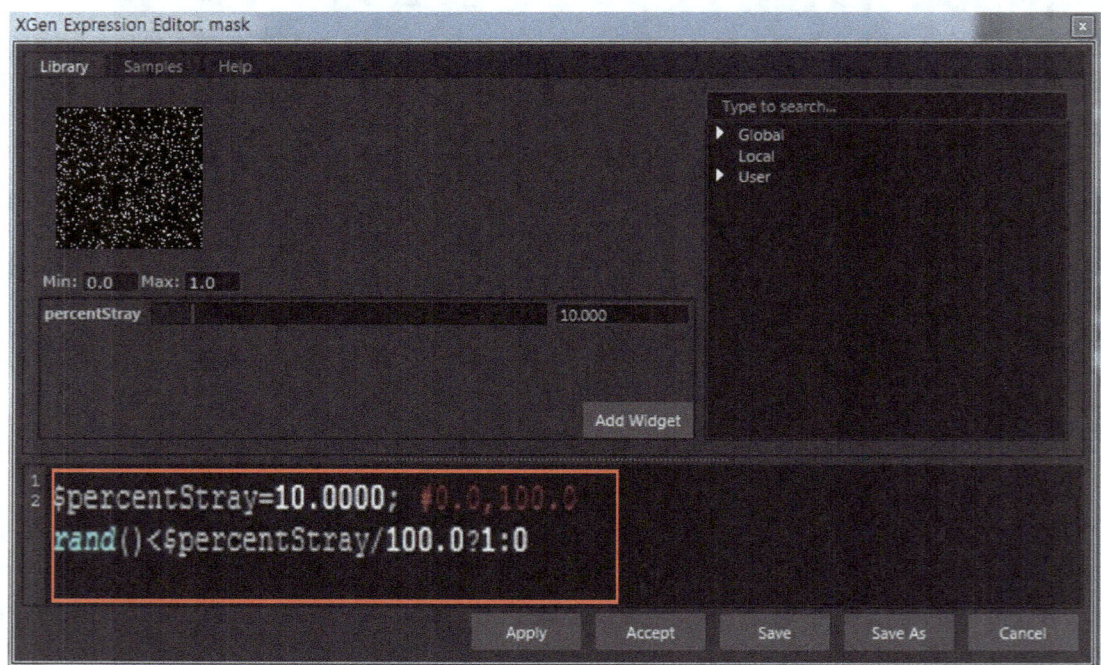

Figure 4.1.4 Expression

This second method allows more flexibility in controlling the stray percentage for each modifier. After adding the expression, a slider will appear next to the mask attribute, which you can adjust for the desired effect.

Page | 103

Coil:

The Coil modifier is used to create wavy hair, adding volume and texture. Apply the same stray hair expression as you did for the Noise modifier. Open the Coil Mask expression editor and paste the expression. Adjust the Mask attribute to control the amount of coiled stray hair.

In the Coil Modifier's settings, set the **Count Scale** graph's **R** and **T** circle values to 0.5. This is the point where the coil begins to curve. Experiment with moving the circles up and down to observe how the coil deforms. The **Radius Scale** controls the coil's amplitude, so try raising the middle of the graph to add more volume to the hair.

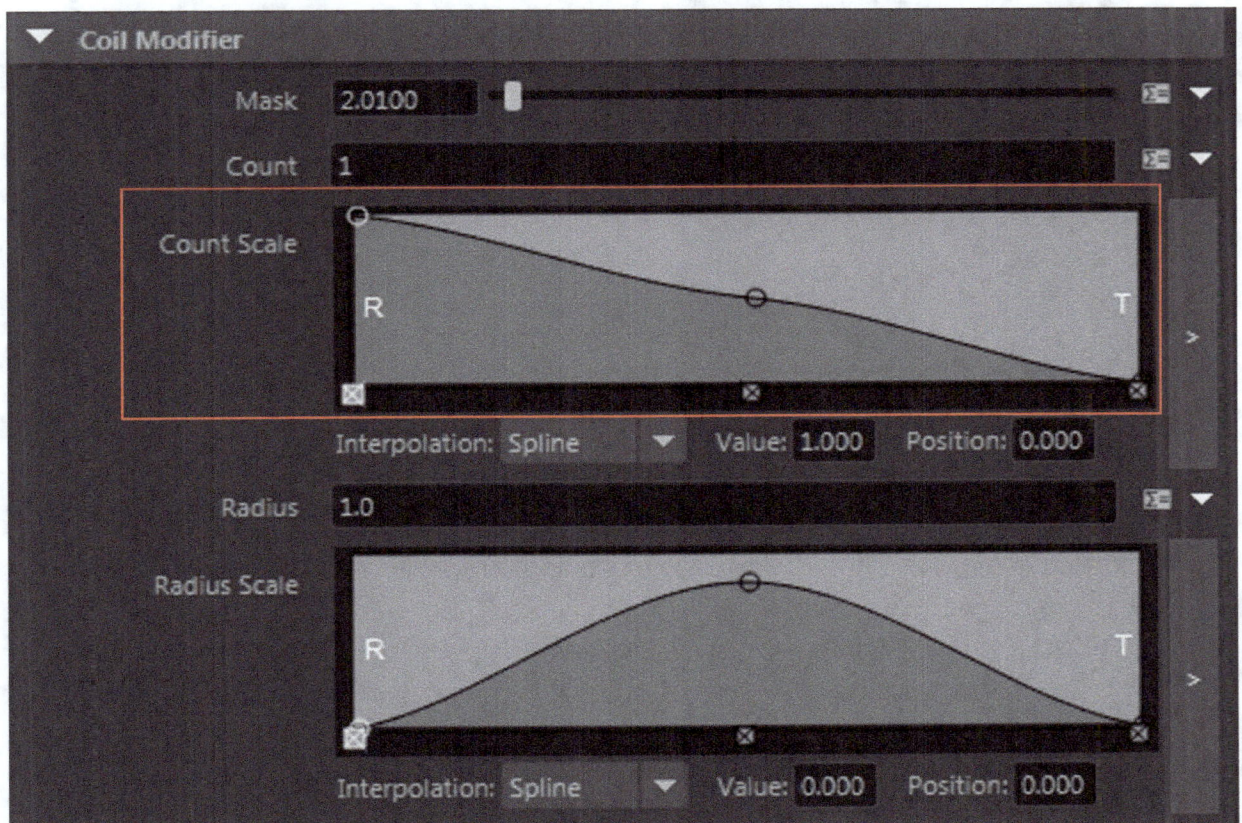

Figure 4.1.5 Coil Modifier: Count Scale

Cut:

For the top hair, we won't be applying the Cut modifier, as the hair is tucked under the back bun and the tips won't be visible. However, for areas where trimming is necessary, set the Cut modifier to randomize the trimming effect for a more natural look. For example, using rand(0,1) trims the hair randomly from 0 to 1 unit from the tip, and you can exceed this range for more dramatic trims.

Final Results:

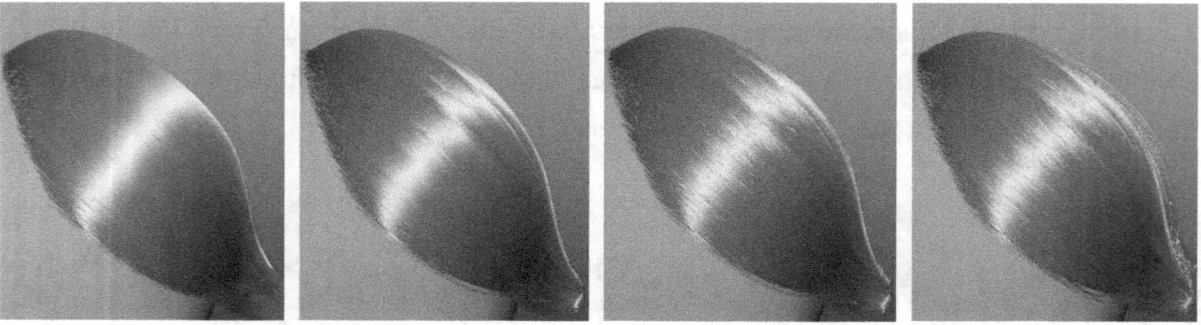

Figure 4.1.6   From left to right: Without modifiers, With Clumping, With Noise, With Coil

4.2 Modifiers: Braid Hair

For braid hair, we will use similar modifiers: **Clumping**, **Noise**, and **Coil**. The process mirrors what we applied to the top hair, but with adjustments for the specific needs of braided styles.

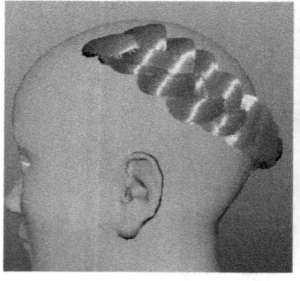 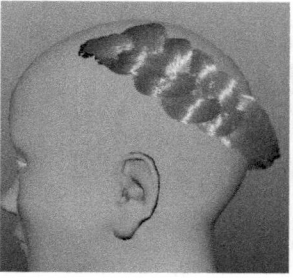 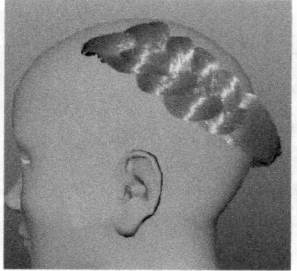 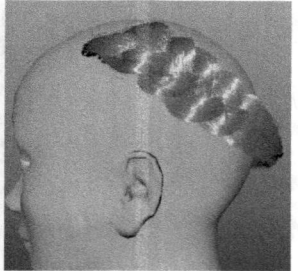

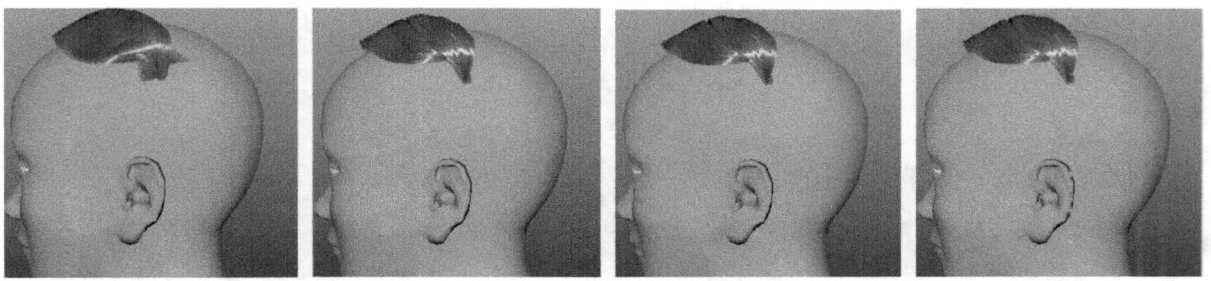

Figure 4.2.1 From left to right: Without modifiers, With Clumping, With Noise, With Coil

Repeat the process for additional braid sections if needed, ensuring that each section has its own refined clumping, noise, and coil modifiers.

4.3 Modifiers: Other Hair Descriptions

Mod fiers such as **Clumping, Noise, Coil,** and occasionally **Cut** will be applied similarly across various hair descriptions like Side Hair, Bangs, Low Side Hair, Long Hair, and more. The key is to adjust the parameters and graph settings for each unique hair style to achieve the desired look.

For each section, consider the following:

- Start with broad clumps and then refine into smaller sections.
- Use Noise and Coil modifiers to add texture and volume.
- Adjust the Mask and attribute settings to control stray hairs or targeted areas.
- Use Cut depending on whether the tips of the hair are visible.

4. Applying Modifiers in XGen

Final Results for Various Descriptions

Side Hair

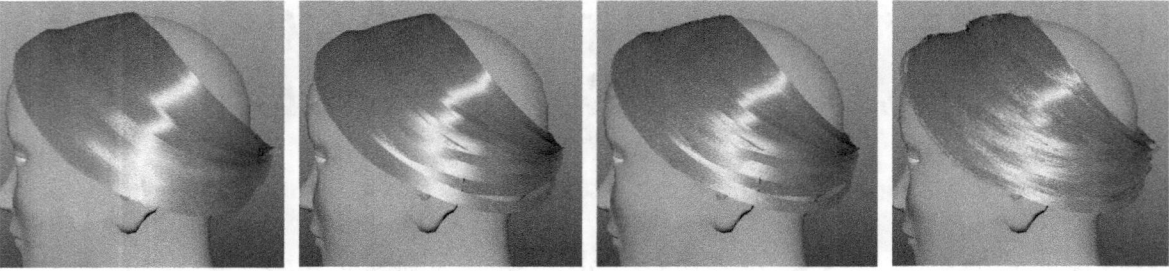

Figure 4.3.1 From left to right: Without modifiers, With Clumping, With Noise, With Coil

Bangs

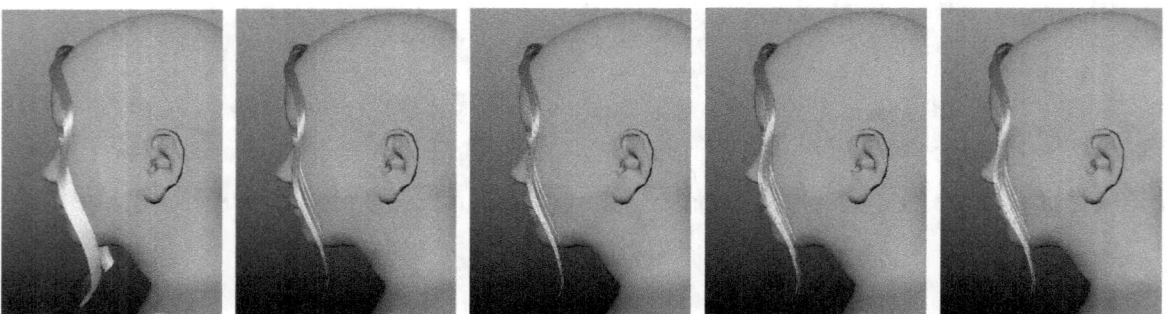

Figure 4.3.2 From left to right: Without modifiers, With Clumping, With Noise, With Coil, With Cut

Low Side Hair

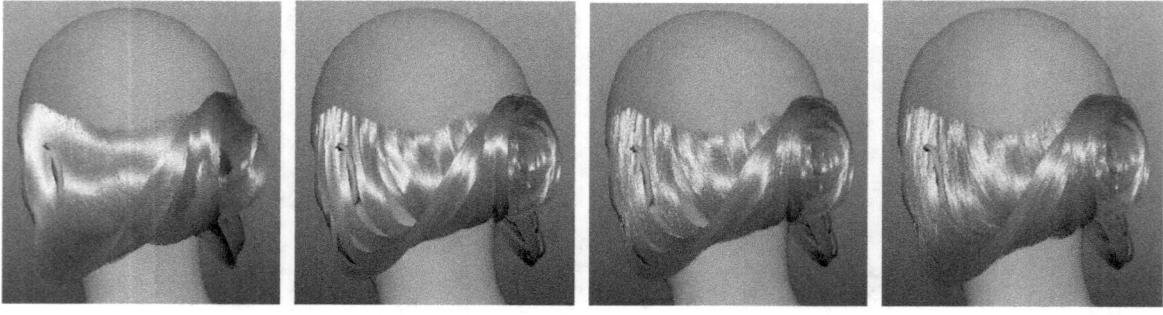

Figure 4.3.3 From left to right: Without modifiers, With Clumping, With Noise, With Coil

Long Hair

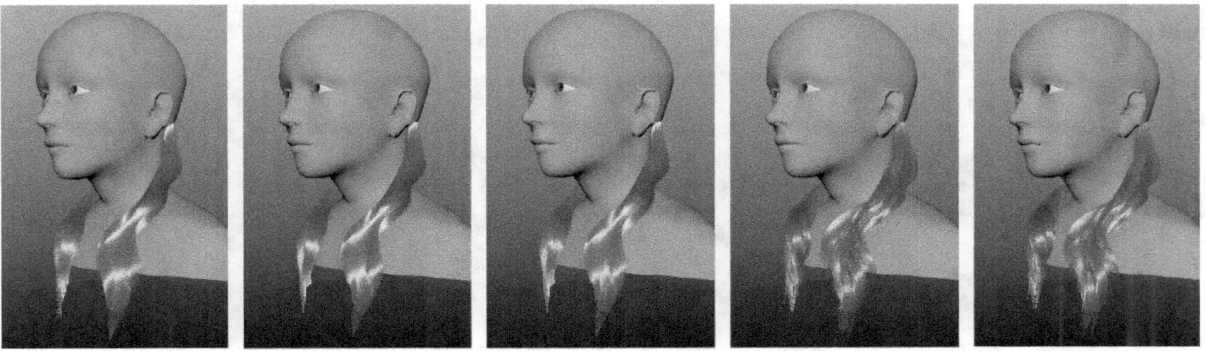

Figure 4.3.4 From left to right: Without modifiers, With Clumping, With Noise, With Coil, With Cut

Long Hair Back

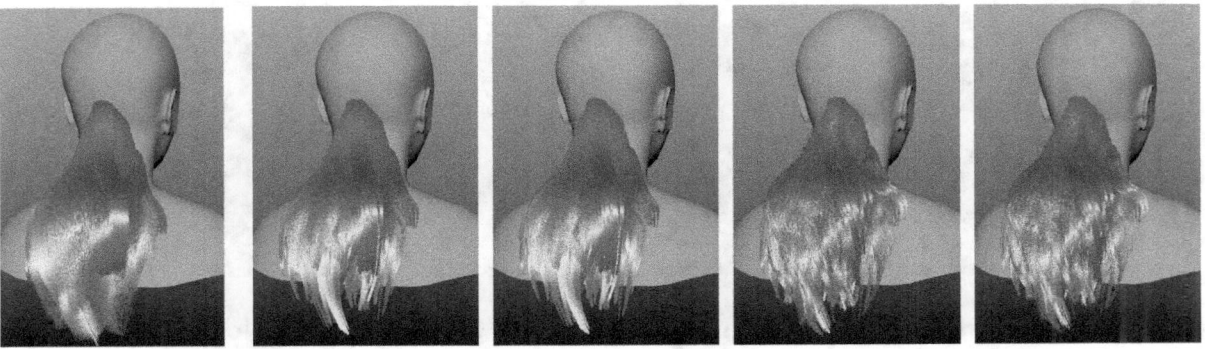

Figure 4.3.5 From left to right: Without modifiers, With Clumping, With Noise, With Coil, With Cut

Bun

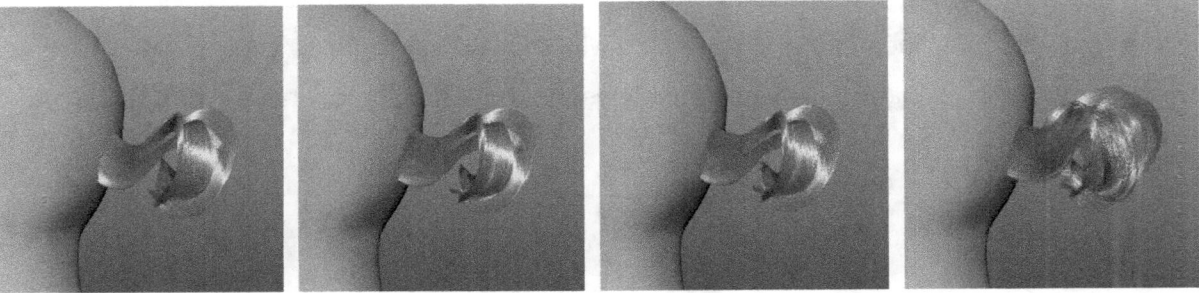

Figure 4.3.6 From left to right: Without modifiers, With Clumping, With Noise, With Coil

Messy Hair Back

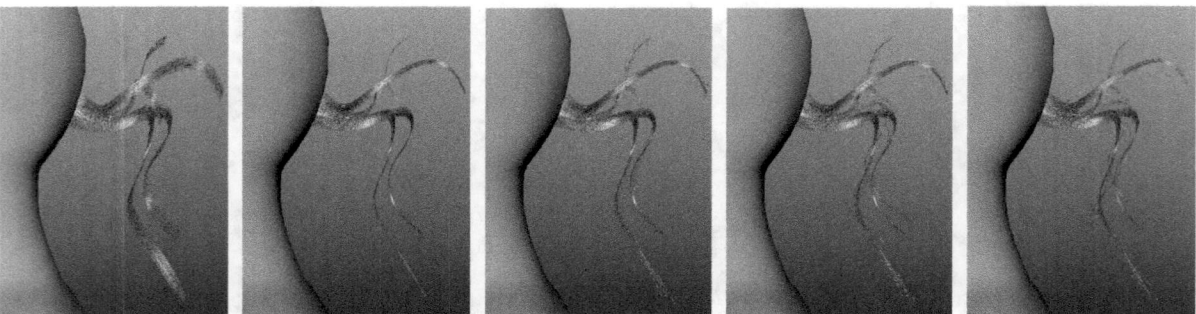

Figure 4.3.7 From left to right: Without modifiers, With Clumping, With Noise, With Coil, With Cut

Flyaway Hair

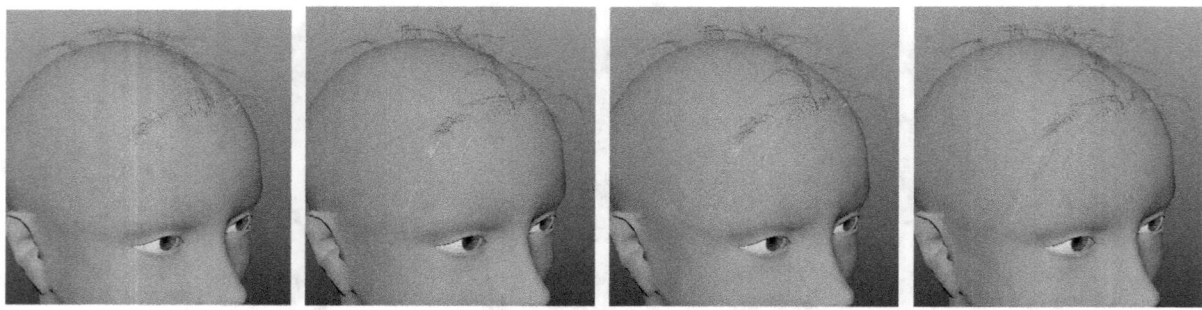

Figure 4.3.8 From left to right: Without modifiers, With Clumping, With Noise, With Coil

Each description requires careful attention to detail to ensure that the modifiers produce realistic and cohesive hair styling across the entire character.

By following these guidelines and experimenting with the various settings, you can use XGen modifiers to craft dynamic and believable hairstyles that enhance the overall appearance of your characters.

XGen Essentials: Long Hair Creation with Splines in Maya

5. Lighting and Shading XGen Hair

Adding lights and rendering can be a time-consuming process, especially when visualizing complex hair textures. In this chapter, we'll use Arnold for lighting and shading, which is a powerful and easy-to-use tool for creating realistic lighting and hair shaders. Before diving into the lighting process, simply assign an **aiStandardSurface** shader to the head geometry to get started.

5.1 Setting Up the Render Camera

1) **Render Settings**
   Open the Render Settings window by navigating to **Windows > Rendering Editors > Render Settings**. Under the **Common** tab, set the Image **Size > Presets** to your desired output resolution (e.g., HD_720, HD_1080, or custom settings).

2) **Create a Render Camera**
   Go to **Create > Cameras > Camera** to set up a render camera. With the camera selected, choose **Panels > Look Through Selected** in the panel menus to adjust the camera's position for your render output. Lock the camera attributes to prevent accidental movement. Select the camera, then in the Channel Box, highlight all the translate, rotate, and scale attributes. Right-click and choose **Lock Selected**. Using **View > Camera Settings > Resolution Gate** will help you see the render region and preview how the final shot will look.

5. Adding Lights and Shaders

3) **Create a Turntable**

   For a turntable animation, go to **Windows > Settings/Preferences > Preferences** and under **Settings > Animation**, set Default in tangents and Default out tangent to Linear. Group the camera using **Ctrl+G**, then go to frame 1 and set a key for the group's Y rotation. At frame 241, set the Y rotation value to 360. Check the keys in the **Windows > Animation Editors > Graph Editor** to ensure they are set to linear tangents.

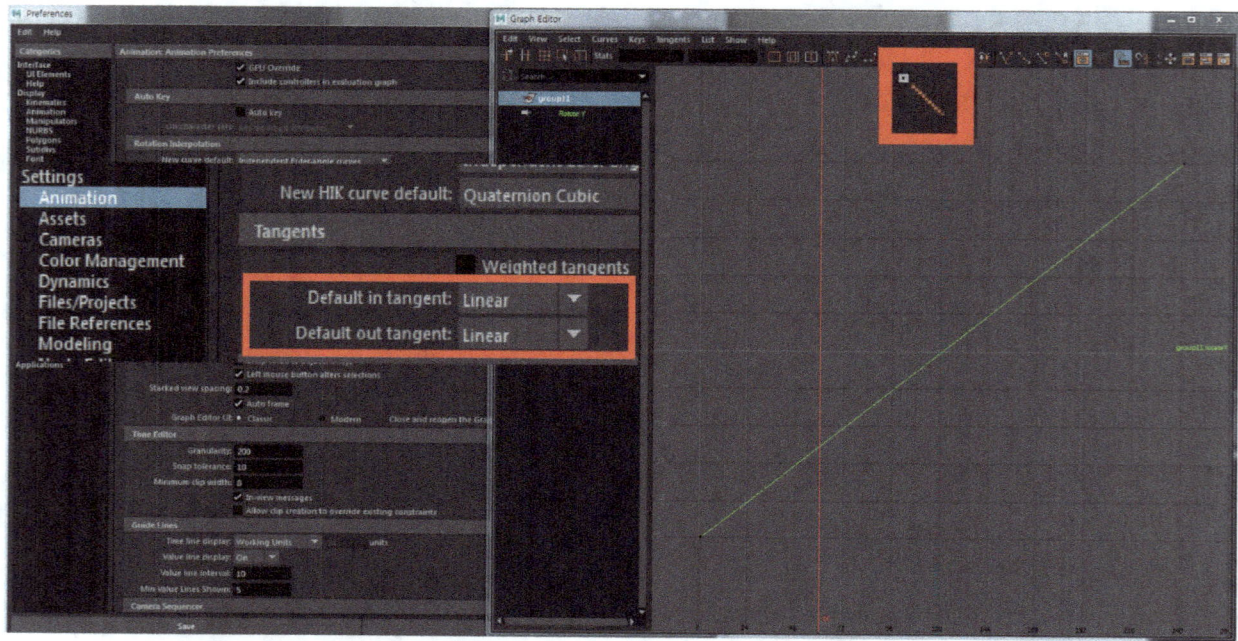

Figure 5.1.1 Setting Animation

5.2 Adding Lights

1) **HDRI Lighting**

   To create natural reflections on the hair, you'll need to add an HDRI map to the scene. Many websites offer free HDRI maps, such as:

   - ✓ hdrihaven.com
   - ✓ texturehaven.com
   - ✓ hdrmaps.com
   - ✓ poliigon.com

Hide all the hair elements by selecting the top collection node in the **Outliner** and hiding it. Also, hide the scalp geometry and other objects, leaving only the human head geometry visible to properly visualize the light effect.

Create a **Skydome Light** by going to **Arnold > Lights > Skydome Light**. In the Attribute Editor **aiSkyDomeLightShape** tab, click the checker icon next to the color attributes and select **File** from the **Create Render Node** window. Open and load an HDRI map that best suits your scene. Rotate the skydome light on the Y-axis to adjust the lighting direction. To prevent the HDRI background from showing in the final render, go to the **aiSkyDomeLightShape** tab, expand the **Visibility** section, and set the **Camera** attribute to 0 (Figure 5.2.2).

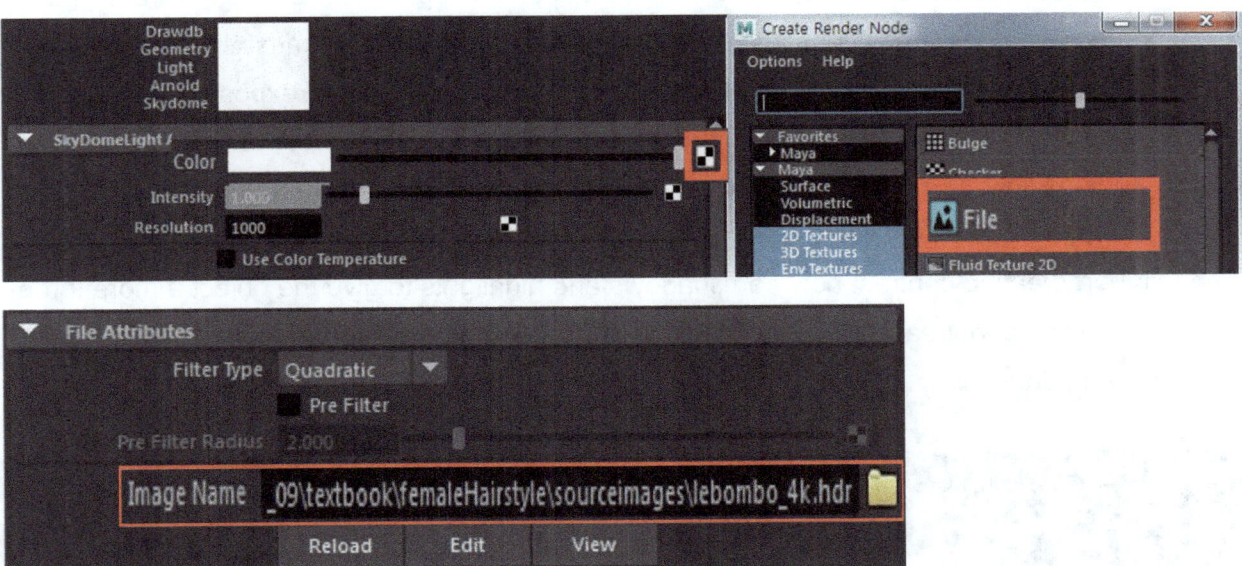

Figure 5.2.1 Setting Up the Skydome Light

5. Adding Lights and Shaders

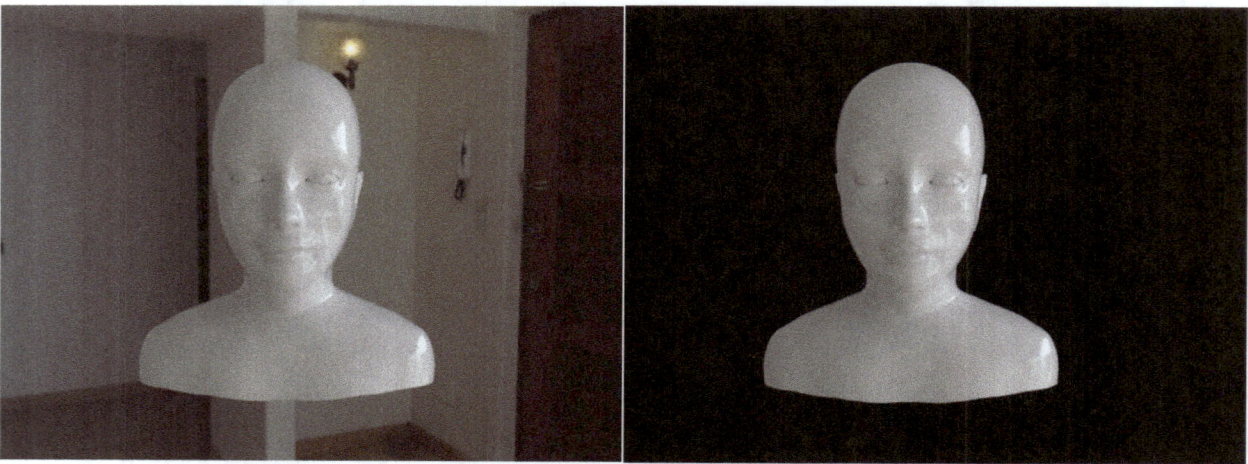

Figure 5.2.2 Visiblity > Camera set to 1 (left) and 0 (right)

2) **Area Lights**

Next, add two **Area Lights** to enhance the aesthetic appeal of your scene. Area lights create smoother transitions in lighting compared to directional or mesh lights. Increase the exposure of the area lights to brighten the shot, but avoid overexposing the scene. A good lighting setup should show a gradient from black to white without washed-out areas. Adding slight color variations to the light sources can also help create more depth and interest. Position the lights so that one side of the head geometry is brighter than the other, creating contrast between shadows and highlights to give the object a more three-dimensional appearance (Figure 5.2.3).Once your lights are set up, unhide the hair descriptions.

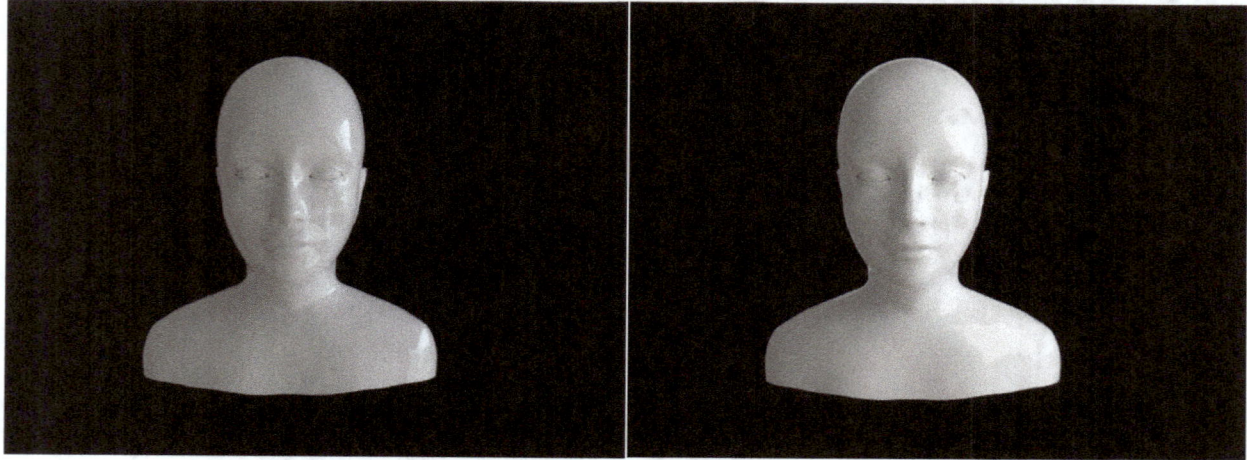

Figure 5.2.3 Without Area Lights (left) and With Area Lights (right)

5.3 Adding Shaders

1) **aiStandardHair Shader**

   Assign an **aiStandard Hair** shader to the XGen hair. Choose **Windows > Rendering Editors > Hypershade** to open the hypershade window. In the work area, press tab and add an **aiStandard Hair** shader. Select the collection or description from the outliner to apply the **aiStandard Hair** shader. Move your cursor to the **aiStandard Hair** shader, right-click, and choose **Assign Material To Viewport Selection**. This physically-based shader allows for realistic hair with just a few adjustments. For detailed information, refer to the Arnold for Maya User Guide. Here, we'll cover the most commonly used attributes:

   Color:

   - **Base:** Controls the brightness of the hair.
   - **Base Color:** Used for applying custom colors or textures. When applying a specific color, set Melanin to 0.
   - **Melanin:** Produces natural hair colors.
   - **Melanin Redness:** Set to 1 for red hues, and 0 for paler colors.
   - **Melanin Randomize:** Adds variation to melanin-based hair colors, ranging from 0 (white) to 1 (black).

   Specular:

   - **Roughness:** Controls the sharpness of specular highlights. Lower values create sharper, shinier highlights (wet/oily hair), while higher values produce softer, duller highlights (dry/matte effect).
   - **IOR:** Controls the strength of reflections; lower values enhance forward scattering, while higher values increase reflection intensity.
   - **Shift:** Adjusts the angle of specular reflections along the hair strands. For realistic results, use values between 0 and 10.

   Tint: Multiplies with the primary color to create non-realistic, artistic effects.

5. Adding Lights and Shaders

Diffuse: Avoid adjusting this for realistic hair shaders.

Emission: Used for artistic purposes.

- **Opacity:** Adds realism at the cost of increased render time. Ensure **Opaque** is turned off when applying this. Setting a black color in the **Opacity** attribute increases render time but creates smoother transitions.

Advanced

- **Indirect Diffuse:** Controls the amount of indirect diffuse light received by the scene.
- **Indirect Specular:** Controls the amount of indirect specular light received by the scene.

2) **Advanced Shaders**

To add color variety to the hair, it is better to connect a ramp shader to the **aiStandard Hair** shader. While **Melanin Randomize** can create random hair strand colors, it may lose color consistency during animations. To avoid this, apply an expression to achieve a similar effect without losing consistency.

- **Ramp Texture Node**
  Adding Colors
  To add colors to the hair, select the **aiStandard Hair** shader and click the checker icon next to either the **Base Color** or **Melanin** attribute. You can use either of these options to apply color to the hair, but ensure that when adjusting the **Melanin**, the **Base Color** is set to white. Conversely, when adjusting the **Base Color**, set the **Melanin** to 0. In this example, we'll apply a ramp texture to the **Melanin** attribute.
- **Applying the Ramp Texture**
  Click the checker icon next to the **Melanin** attribute. This will open the **Create Render Node** window. Select the **Ramp** texture node. In the channel box, adjust the first and second color points on the ramp graph to define the root and tip colors of the hair. If you're applying this to the **Melanin** attribute, note that white in the ramp graph represents black hair, and black represents white hair. For precise control, under **Ramp Node > Ramp Attributes > Selected Color**, click the color space and adjust the **V**

value in the HSV range to set the desired hair color (e.g., 0 for white, 0.2 for blond, 0.5 for brown, and 1 for black). These values will correspond to the melanin levels in the hair.

- **Adding Noise**

  To create more variation in the blending of colors, add **Noise** and **Noise Frequency** under the **Ramp Attributes**. This will introduce irregularities in the color transitions, making the hair appear more natural.

- **Refining Color Blending**

  You can further refine the color blending by moving the color points left and right on the ramp graph. This will adjust where the root and tip colors blend, allowing for more precise control over the color distribution in the hair.

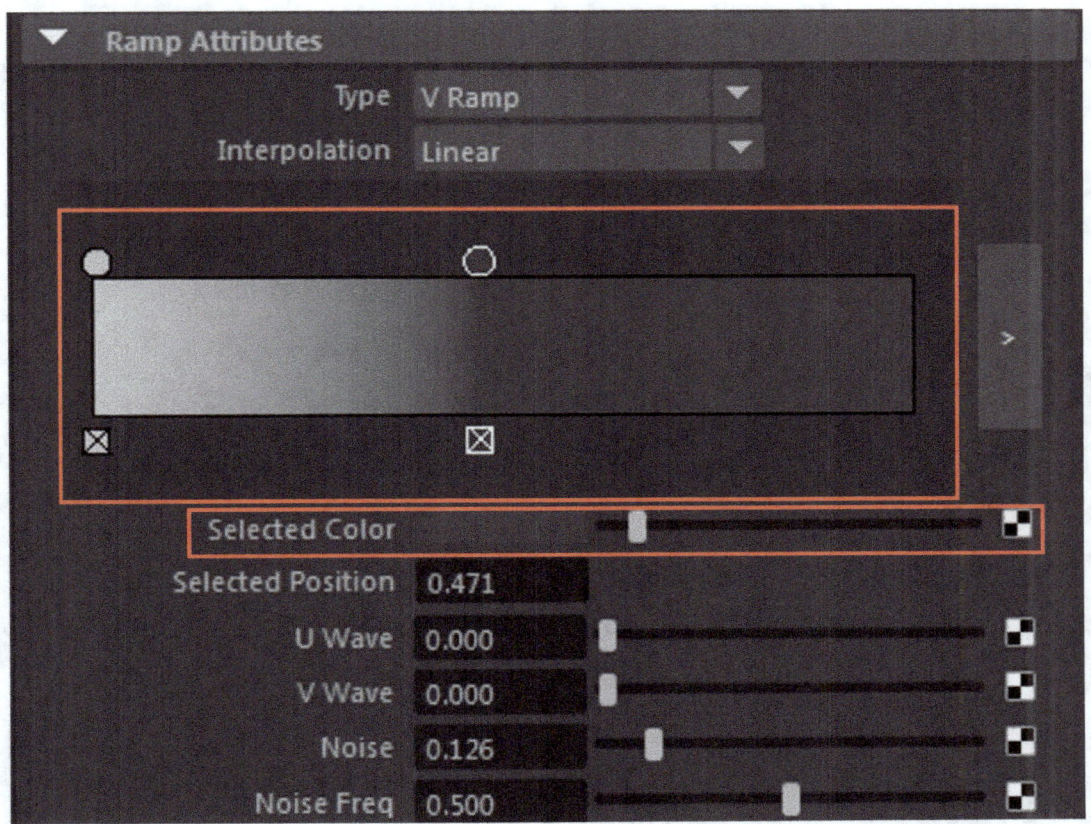

Figure 5.3.1 Color Blending

3) **aiUserDataFloat:**

   To paint and customize texture colors or apply varying color percentages to different

5. Adding Lights and Shaders

parts of the hair, you'll need to create an **aiUserDataColor** or **aiUserDataFloat** node. In this section, we'll focus on adding randomized color to the base hair color using expressions.

- **Creating a Custom Shader Parameter**
  Start by navigating to **XGen > Preview/Output > Custom Shader Parameters**. Here, under the **Name** attribute, type hairFloat. This will create a new custom parameter for controlling the hair color.
- **Setting the Float Attribute**
  Set the parameter type to **float** and click the plus (+) sign to the right. This will generate the float parameter called hairFloat.
- **Adding an Expression**

Next, click on the expression icon to open the expression editor. In the bottom panel, input the following expression:

$a=10.0000; #0.0,100.0
rand()<$a/100?rand(0.0,0.5):0.2

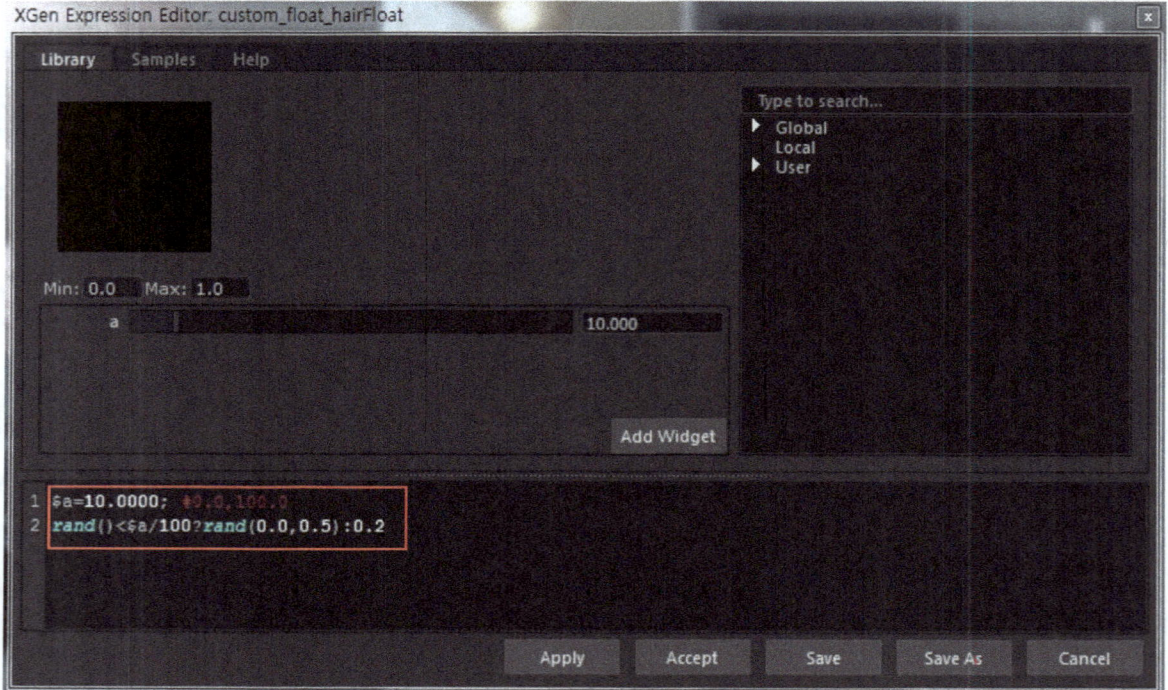

Figure 5.3.2 Expression

This expression introduces a 10% chance of generating a random color between white (0) and brown (0.5). The main hair color will default to blonde (0.2), but you can adjust these values to suit your desired hair color variation.

- **Assigning the Color to the Ramp**

    Go to the ramp attributes and select the first color. Click the checker icon next to the **Selected Color** attribute. This will open the **Create Render Node** window. Choose **Arnold** from the list, type "aiUserDataFloat", and select it. Then, type "hairFloat" in the attribute to the node matching the **Custom Shader Parameters** name.

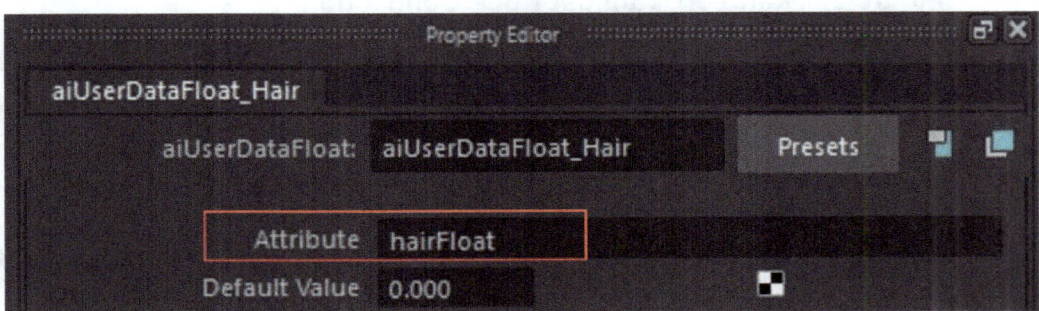

    Figure 5.3.3 aiUserDataFloat Node

- **Rendering the Result**

    Once everything is set up, check your render view to see if the randomized color is applied correctly. You should notice varying shades of hair color based on the expression you've added.

5. Adding Lights and Shaders

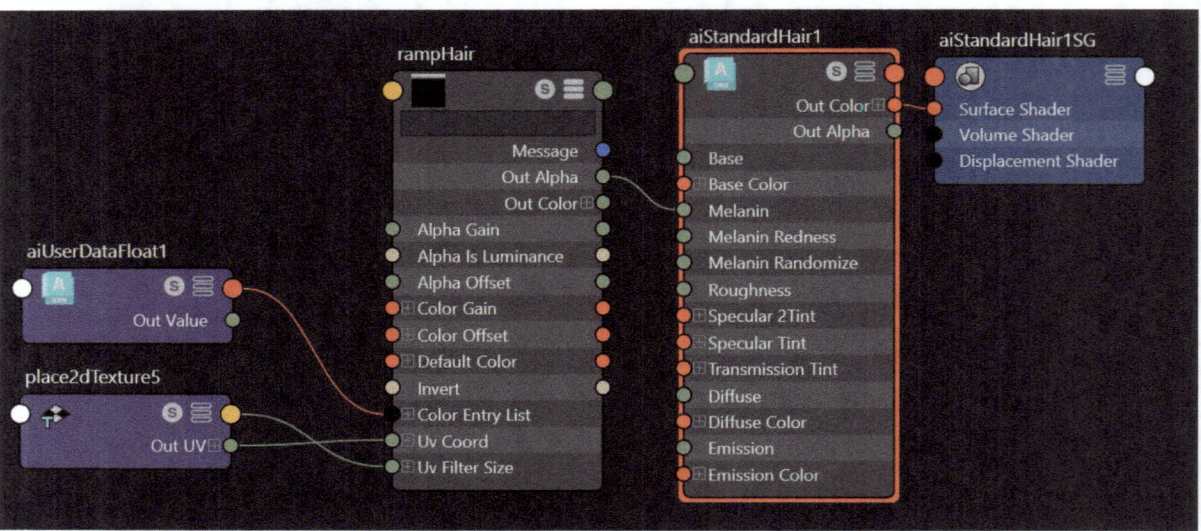

Figure 5.3.4 aiUserDataFloat Node Connection

Adjusting Tip Color with aiSubstract Node

With the root hair color now controlled by an expression, we need to ensure that the tip color interacts with the root color as well. This can be done by adding an **aiSubstract** node to offset the tip color based on the root color.

1) **Creating an aiSubstract Node**
   In **Windows>Rendering Editors>Hypershade,** create a new **aiSubstract** node. Press tab and type "aiSubstract". This node will help us apply an offset color to the hair tips.

2) **Connecting the Nodes**
   Connect the output **Out Value** from the **aiUserDataFloat** node to the **Input 1R, 1G, and 1B** channels of the **aiSubstract** node. This connection will link the root color to the subtraction process.

3) **Setting the Tip Color**
   Next, connect the **Out Color** from the **aiSubstract** node to the second color on the ramp Color **Entry List[1]>Color**, which represents the tip color. This will allow the tip color to be affected by the offset you apply.

Page | 119

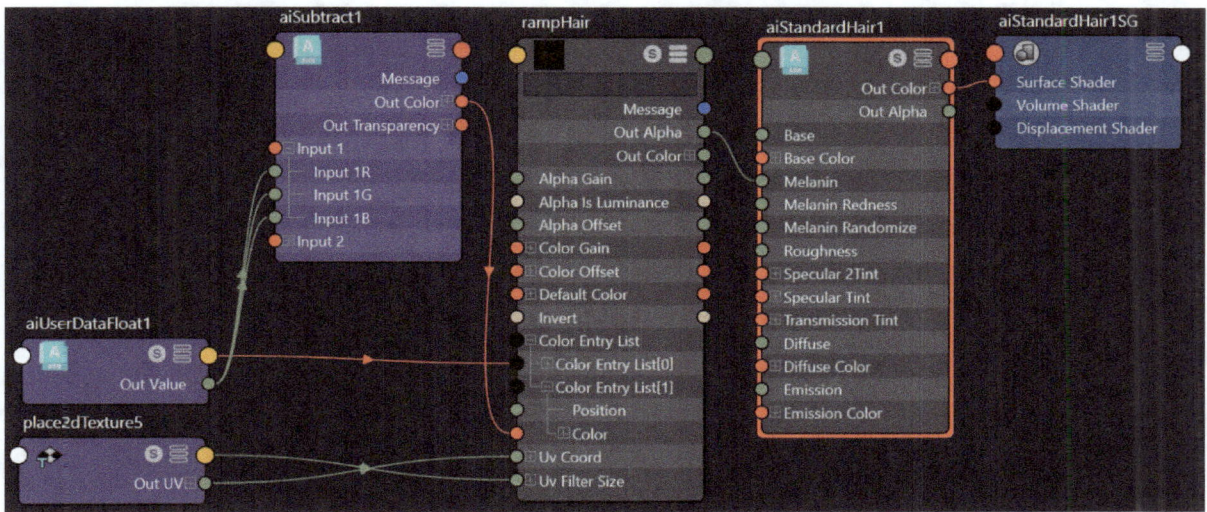

Figure 5.3.5 aiSubtract Node

4) **Fine-Tuning the Tip Color**

At this point, the tip color will initially match the root color because no offset has been set. To adjust this, modify the **input2** color space in the **aiSubstract** node until the desired variation in the tip color is achieved.

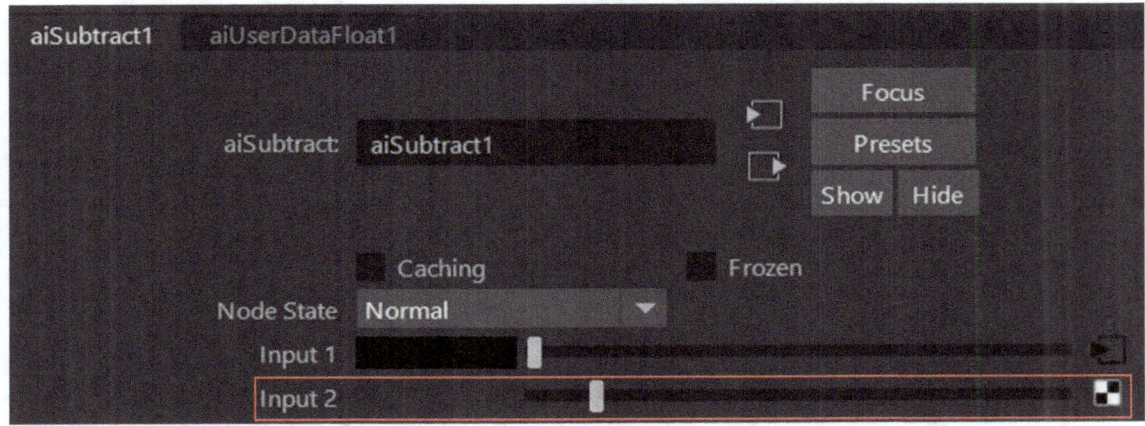

Figure 5.3.6 Tuning the Tip Color

5.4 Render Settings

Rendering hair in XGen requires careful attention to detail, especially when it comes to sampling and lighting. Proper render settings can dramatically impact the quality of your hair renders, reducing noise and optimizing performance. This section will guide you through setting up your render settings for XGen hair, with a focus on achieving clean, realistic results efficiently.

Importance of Specular Sampling

When rendering hair, specular reflections play a crucial role in achieving realistic results. Hair tends to reflect light in complex ways, so increasing specular sampling is essential for reducing noise and ensuring smooth, natural highlights.

Tips for Render Tests

Rendering hair can be resource-intensive, so optimizing your render tests is key to saving time. Here are some tips for conducting render tests effectively:

1) **Lower Resolution for Testing**

    To speed up your render tests, reduce the resolution and image size as much as possible while still being able to evaluate the hair's appearance. Open the **Windows > Rendering Editors > Render Settings**, expand the **Image Size** section, and set the resolution presets to 640x480 or 320x240. This will allow you to quickly preview the hair without waiting for full-resolution renders.

2) **Arnold Renderer > Sampling Settings**

    In the **Arnold Renderer** tab, adjust the sampling settings for faster test renders:

    - **Camera (AA)**: Set to 2
    - **Diffuse**: Set to 1
    - **Specular**: Set to 2
    - **Transmission**: Set to 1
    - **SSS (Subsurface Scattering)**: Set to 1

- **Volume Indirect**: Set to 1

3) **Ray Depth Settings**

   Also in the **Arnold Renderer** tab, under **Ray Depth**, adjust the following:

   - **Diffuse**: Set to 1
   - **Specular**: Set to 1
   - **Transmission**: Set to 1
   - **Volume**: Set to 0

4) **Using Arnold RenderView**

   Open the **Arnold RenderView** (**Arnold > Open Arnold RenderView**) and set it to render from your camera. This gives you a focused view of your render, ensuring you're evaluating the final composition.

5) **Test Resolution**

   In the **Arnold RenderView**, you can further speed up rendering by setting the test resolution to a lower percentage. Go to **View > Test Resolution** and choose a lower percentage to reduce the render time.

6) **Using Crop Region**

   For quick checks of specific hair areas, use the crop region tool. Hold down **Shift + Left Mouse Button** (LMB) and drag to select a region. This will render only the selected area, allowing you to focus on particular sections without rendering the entire frame.

Sampling Settings Overview

Correct sampling settings are crucial for reducing noise in your hair renders. Here's a breakdown of the main sampling parameters:

1) **Camera (AA):**

   Controls the quality of motion blur and depth of field. The number of Camera (AA) samples is multiplied by the square of the value you input. Higher values lead to higher-quality renders but significantly increase render times.

2) **Diffuse**:

   Increase this value if you notice noise in indirect diffuse lighting areas, such as shadows or bounced light.

3) **Specular**:

   Increase this if your render shows noise in specular highlights, which are particularly important for hair reflections.

4) **Transmission**:

   Increase this value if you encounter noise in transparent objects, such as glass or thin materials that light passes through.

5) **Subsurface Scattering (SSS)**:

   If you're using SSS for materials like skin, increase this value to reduce noise in those areas.

6) **Light Samples**:

   Light samples (diffuseDirect and specularDirect) should be increased if you see noise in shadows or direct lighting areas. It's important to test each light individually to see if adjustments are needed.

To further troubleshoot noise issues, you can use **AOV (Arbitrary Output Variables)** for specific sampling tests which can be found under the **AOVs** tab in the **Render Settings**: For this tutorial, we will simply test the four AOVs shown in Figure 5.4.1. Select these from the left column and move them to the right. Once we set the AOVs on the right, open the Arnold RenderView from the Arnold menu (Arnold > Open Arnold RenderView). On the right side of the Arnold RenderView window, you can easily select the various render passes from the drop-down menu.

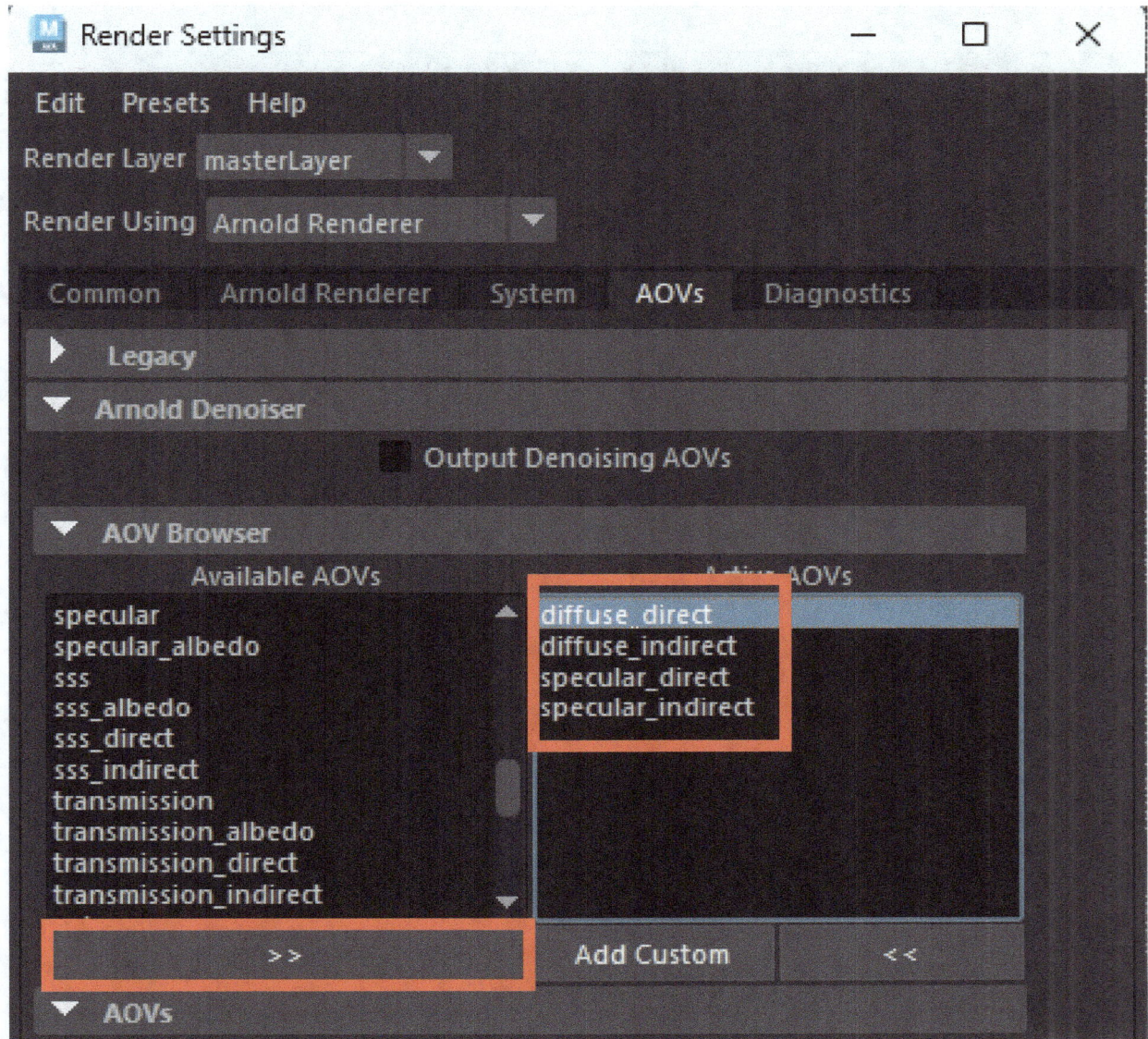

Figure 5.4.1 Render Settings > AOV

Removing Noise in Hair

Reducing noise in hair rendering requires careful adjustments to sampling settings. Below is a guide to help you identify which parameters to adjust based on the type of noise:

5. Adding Lights and Shaders

Sampling	Diffuse (AOV)		Specular(AOV)	
	Direct	Indirect	Direct	Indirect
Diffuse	△	O	X	X
Specular	X	X	O Good but slow	O
Light	O (Area light not effecting the noise, Skydome light samples remove the noise)	X	O direct light areas are removed	X

- **Diffuse Noise**

  If you see noise in diffuse AOV, increase the Diffuse sampling.

- **Specular Noise**

  If the noise is in the specular AOV, adjust the Specular sampling. Direct light areas can also benefit from increasing light samples.

Reflection Test: Comparing Specular Roughness vs IOR

Specular roughness and **Index of Refraction** (IOR) can have a significant impact on the appearance of reflections in your render. Below are examples of different settings and their effects:

1. **Render Settings**

   Camera (AA): 2, Diffuse: 1, Specular: 4, Transmission: 1, SSS: 1, Volume Indirect: 1

2. **Example Comparisons**

- **Roughness: 0.03, IOR: 1.55**

  This setting produces sharp reflections with a low roughness value.

- **Roughness: 0.2, IOR: 1.55**

  Increasing the roughness softens the reflections, giving a more diffused look.

- **Roughness: 0.2, IOR: 2.0**

  A higher IOR increases the reflectivity, creating more pronounced reflections, especially on glossy surfaces.

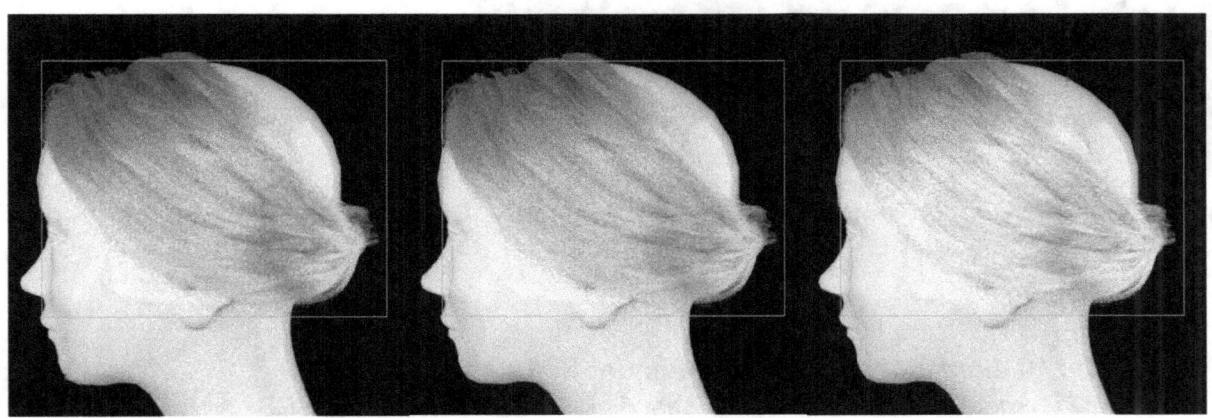

Figure 5.4.2   Figure Roughness:0.03 IOR:1.55(left)   Roughness:0.2 IOR:1.55(mid)   Roughness:0.2   IOR:2.0(right)

Sampling Test Results

Here are results from various sampling tests, demonstrating the impact on render times and quality:

- **Render Settings (Low Quality Render Settings)**

  - Camera (AA): 2, Diffuse: 1, Specular: 2, Transmission: 1, SSS: 1, Volume Indirect: 1
  - **Render Time**: 44 seconds (on a specific computer)

5. Adding Lights and Shaders

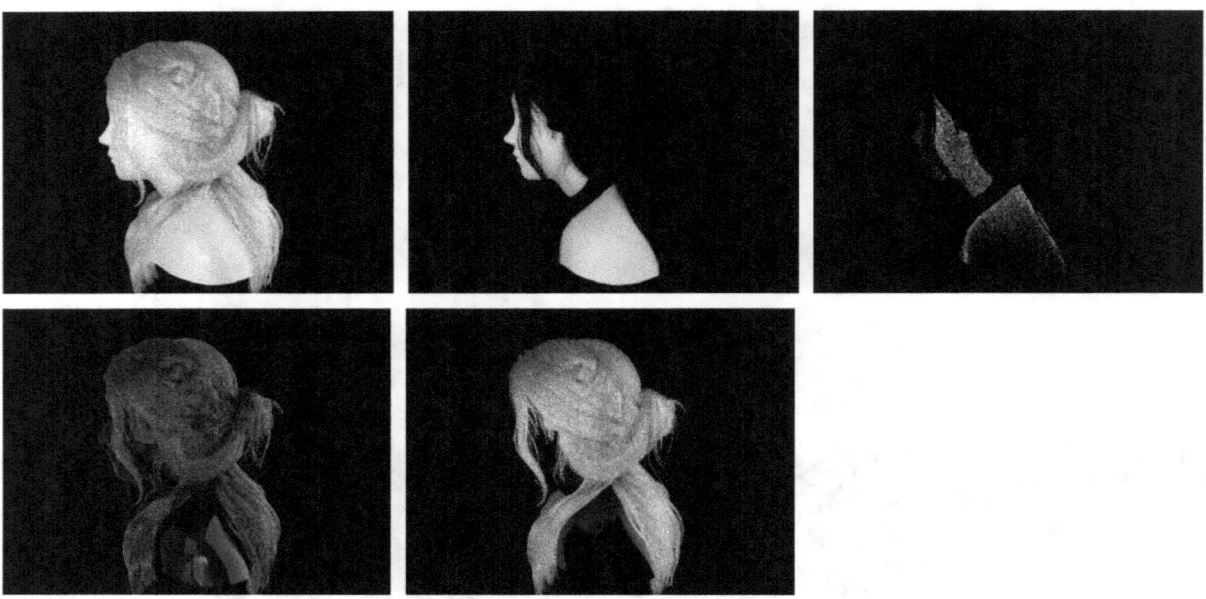

Figure 5.4.3 Low Quality Render Settings. AOV: Beauty, Diffuse Direct, Diffuse Indirect, Specular Direct, Specular Indirect starting from top left to bottom right.

- **Render Settings (Medium Quality Render Settings)**
  - Camera (AA): 4, Diffuse: 3, Specular: 4, Transmission: 1, SSS: 1, Volume Indirect: 1
  - **Render Time**: 12 minutes (on a specific computer)

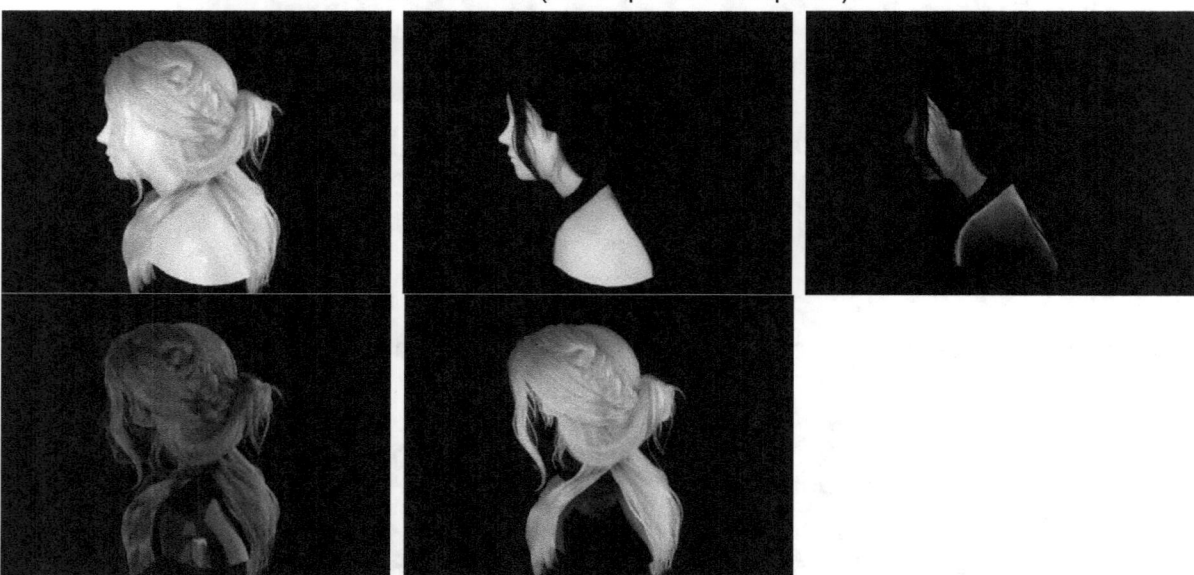

Figure 5.4.4 Medium Quality Render Settings. AOV: Beauty, Diffuse Direct, Diffuse Indirect, Specular Direct, Specular Indirect starting from top left to bottom right.

- **Render Settings (High Quality Render Settings)**
    - Camera (AA): 7, Diffuse: 5, Specular: 6, Transmission: 1, SSS: 1, Volume Indirect: 1
    - **Render Time**: 1 hour 24 minutes (on a specific computer)

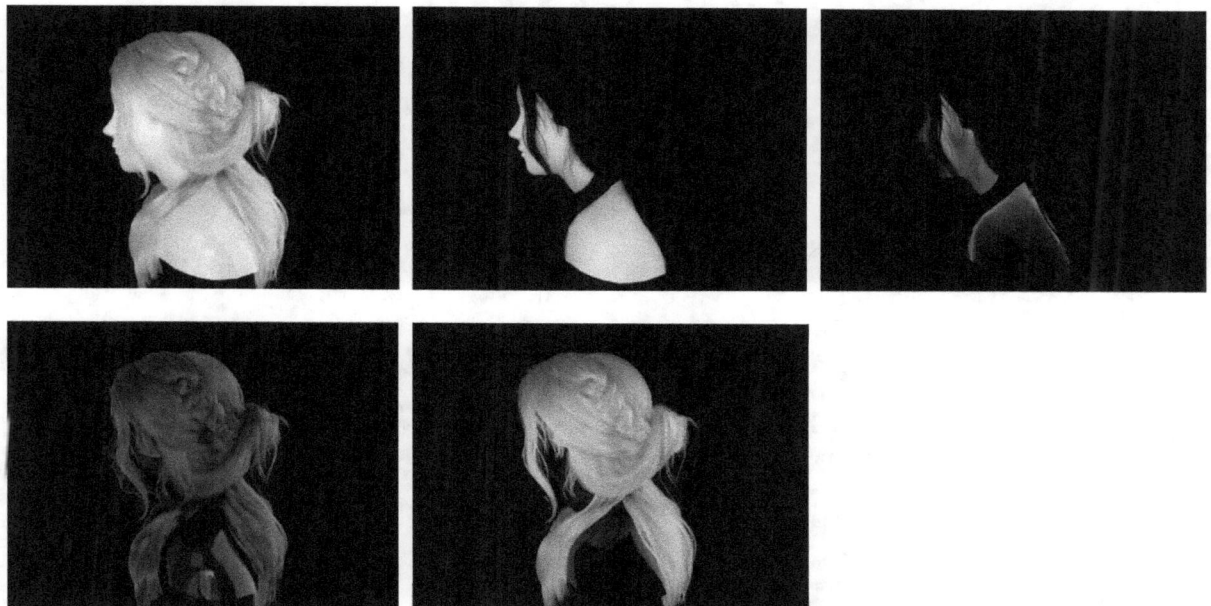

Figure 5.4.5 High Quality Render Settings. AOV: Beauty, Diffuse Direct, Diffuse Indirect, Specular Direct, Specular Indirect starting from top left to bottom right.

These examples highlight the trade-off between render quality and time. Adjust your sampling settings based on the level of detail required for your final output, balancing render quality with practical time constraints.

From the test results, we can see that noise is reduced between Low Quality (Figure 5.4.3) and Medium Quality (Figure 5.4.4) Render Settings. However, the difference between Medium (Figure 5.4.4) and High Quality (Figure 5.4.5) Render Settings is minimal, allowing us to use Medium Quality without spending too much time on High Quality Render Settings, which can be more efficient to work with.

Properly configuring your render settings for XGen hair is crucial to achieving high-quality results while managing render times efficiently. By following the tips and settings in this chapter, you'll be able to create realistic hair with minimized noise and optimal performance for both test and final renders. Experiment with the different parameters and find the balance that works best for your project.

XGen Essentials: Long Hair Creation with Splines in Maya

6. Simulating Hair Movement with XGen

In this chapter, we will explore the two primary approaches to simulating XGen hair in Maya: Top-down and Bottom-up. The top-down approach involves activating the hair system directly from **Primitives**, while the bottom-up method provides more control by using **AnimWire** Modifiers for dynamic curves. We'll dive into both methods, their settings, and how to achieve optimal results for your XGen hair simulations.

Two Types of Hair Simulation

Top-down Approach (Activating the Hair System from **Primitives**):
This method involves generating an aa system from XGen guides. It's quick to set up and efficient for basic simulations.
Bottom-up Approach (Creating an **AnimWire** Modifier for Dynamic Curves):
This approach allows for finer control by introducing dynamic curves via **AnimWire** Modifiers. It's ideal for complex animations where you need more detailed customization.

Initial Simulation Considerations

Before running the simulation, you need to ensure that your settings are optimized for accurate playback. Here are key points to keep in mind:

Playback Settings

Go to **Window > Settings/Preferences > Preferences** and select **Time Slider**.
Set **Playback Speed** to **Play Every Frame** to ensure Maya evaluates every frame accurately. Recommend to lock the **maximum playback speed** to 24 fps to maintain consistency.

Simulation Setup

Run the simulation after setting up the system. If the hair behaves unexpectedly (e.g., bursting out), you may need to adjust the nucleus solver settings for better results.

6.1 Activating the Hair System from Primitives

The top-down method begins by creating an nHair system based on your XGen guides.

Steps to Activate the Hair System
Navigate to the **Primitives > Guide Animation** section and enable the **Use Animation** option. Click **Create Hair System**, set your **NURBS curves**, and press **Make Curves Dynamic**. Finally, select all your simulating output curves from the outliner and press **Attach Hair System** to attach them to your guide curve

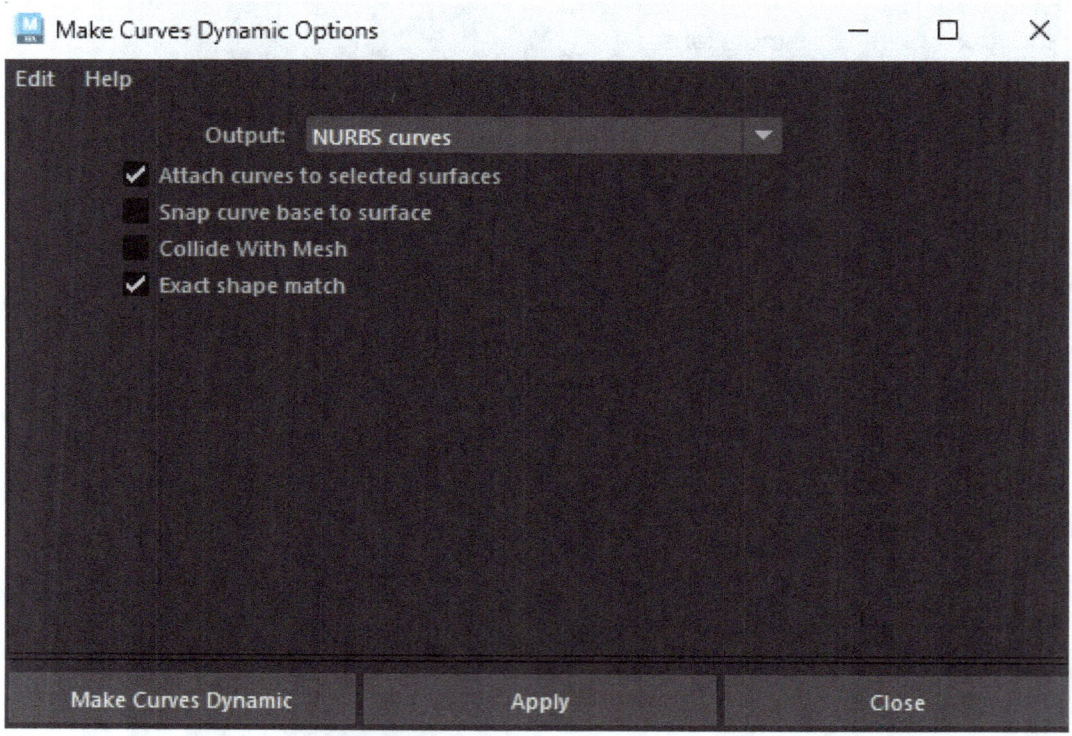

Figure 6.1.1 Hair System Option

Maya will generate an nHair system derived from the guide curves, along with follicles under the **xgGroom** node and an nDynamics **nucleus** node.

Adjusting Simulation Preferences

Before adjusting dynamic properties, select the nucleus solver and adjust the **Space Scale** to align the simulation with Maya's working unit scale. Maya always measures each grid as meters in dynamics. Select the nucleus node, and under **Scale Attributes**, set the **Space Scale** to 0.01. For example, if the head length spans 30 grid units, it should be 30 centimeters, but without adjusting the scale, it will be interpreted as 30 meters.

For test simulations, try lowering the **Substeps** and **Max Collision Iterations**. Later, increase the **Substeps** to 8 and **Max Collision Iterations** to 10 to improve accuracy.

Handling Collisions:

If the hair penetrates the geometry, select the passive object and create a passive collider for the head using **nCloth > Create Passive Collider**.

Adjust dynamic properties such as **Stretch Resistance, Compression Resistance, Damp,** and **Mass** to fine-tune the hair's response to forces like gravity.

Caching the Simulation:

Once the simulation behaves as expected, you should cache the results to improve performance during playback and rendering.

Use an **Alembic Cache** for finalized simulations. Select all the nHair output NURBS curves and go to **Cache > Alembic Cache > Export Selection to Alembic**. Save the cache to your project's cache directory and ensure the time range covers the entire simulation.

After caching, turn off the nucleus solver and disable live mode in XGen, then load the cache file into the **Cache File Name** field. Maya will now reference the cached data, allowing you to scrub through the timeline without recalculating the simulation, which significantly improves performance.

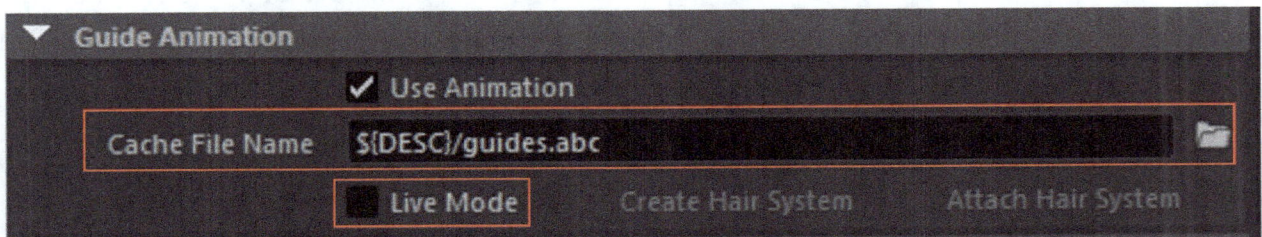

Figure 6.1.2 Alembic Cache

6. Simulation for XGen Hair

6.2 Creating an AnimWire Modifier for Dynamic Curves

The bottom-up approach offers greater customization by controlling individual hair primitives with **AnimWire** Modifiers.

Steps to Create AnimWire Modifier:

In the XGen window, go to the **Modifiers** tab and press **Add New Modifier** and select the **AnimWires** and press **OK**. This will allow you to introduce dynamic curves that control how the hair behaves during the simulation.

Scroll down to the **Control Map** section. Here, you can create new maps to determine which dynamic curves each hair primitive will follow during the simulation.

Select **Clumping** or **Default** under **Control Map**. Clumping maps offer predictable results by generating dynamic curves based on existing clump points.

Generate Dynamic Curves

Once the control maps are set up, turn off the XGen preview to get a clearer view of the geometry.

If you choose **Default**, click the **Create Maps** button to generate points at the locations specified by the control map. From the **Generate Map** Window, choose either **Guide** to match the guide curve or set the **Density > Generate** button to manage your own simulation density, and press **Create** button under **Maps**. These points dictate where the dynamic curves will be placed, affecting how the hair primitives move. I prefer to match the **Clumping** because if you choose **Default** under **Control Map**, the simulation moves based on the **Density**, which ruins the clumping shape you created while animating the character.

After generating the points, click the **Preview Wires** button to see how the dynamic curves will be positioned. This gives you a visual representation of the wires that will drive the hair simulation, allowing you to make any necessary adjustments before proceeding.

Click **Create Hair System** to generate the dynamic curves. Maya will create a hair system node driven by a nucleus solver, along with a set of curves and corresponding follicles at each point. Finally, click Attach Hair System to connect the output simulation curves to XGen. Play the animation and test how the simulation works in your scene.

Adjust the Hair System

The first step is to set Maya's working unit scale under the nucleus solver's **Scale Attributes > Space Scale**, based on the size of the head.

Next, configure the hair system's **Dynamic Properties**, such as **Stretch Resistance, Compression Resistance, Mass**, and **Damp**, to make the hair lighter and more responsive.

Extra Steps for Better Collision

If we set up a collider by selecting the body or the colliding object, go to the **FX** menu and select **nCloth > Create Passive Collider**, the XGen guides will interact with the colliding mesh. However, the XGen primitives themselves cannot detect the collision mesh, which causes penetration issues in some parts of the hair. To resolve this, we'll add a **Collision** modifier. This allows the XGen primitives to directly detect and resolve collisions with the mesh. For the **Collision** modifier to work effectively, an Alembic cache of the collision mesh is required.

Creating the Alembic Cache

First, turn off the XGen preview to focus on the geometry.

Select the body or the collision geometry, then navigate to **Cache > Alembic Cache > Export Selection to Alembic.**

Save the cache in the cache directory and ensure the time range covers the full timeline.

Once Maya caches the head geometry animation, add the **Collision** modifier from the **Add Modifier Window (Modifiers** tab **> Add new Modifier)** to reference this new cache file. Then, upload the collision alembic cache file. This will allow the hair to collide properly with the mesh, greatly improving the simulation.

Figure 6.2.1 Applying Alembic Cache to Collision Modifier

Re-Caching After Changes:

6. Simulation for XGen Hair

Remember, if you make any changes to the head geometry animation, you will need to regenerate the Alembic cache to ensure the collision calculations remain accurate.

Fine-Tune the Simulation:

Adjust the **Magnitude Scale** ramp. Set the point at the root to zero and the tip to one. This ensures that each primitive retains the shape of its guide at the root, then gradually interpolates to the shape of the nHair curves towards the tip (Figure 6.2.2).

This provides better control over the simulation and prevents hair penetration issues.

If certain regions of the hair need to maintain their shape (such as bangs), paint a mask with varying shades of gray to control the motion of specific hair regions while still allowing for subtle animation. To achieve this, create a map from the **Anim Wire Modifier > Mask** to limit the influence of the dynamic curves in those areas.

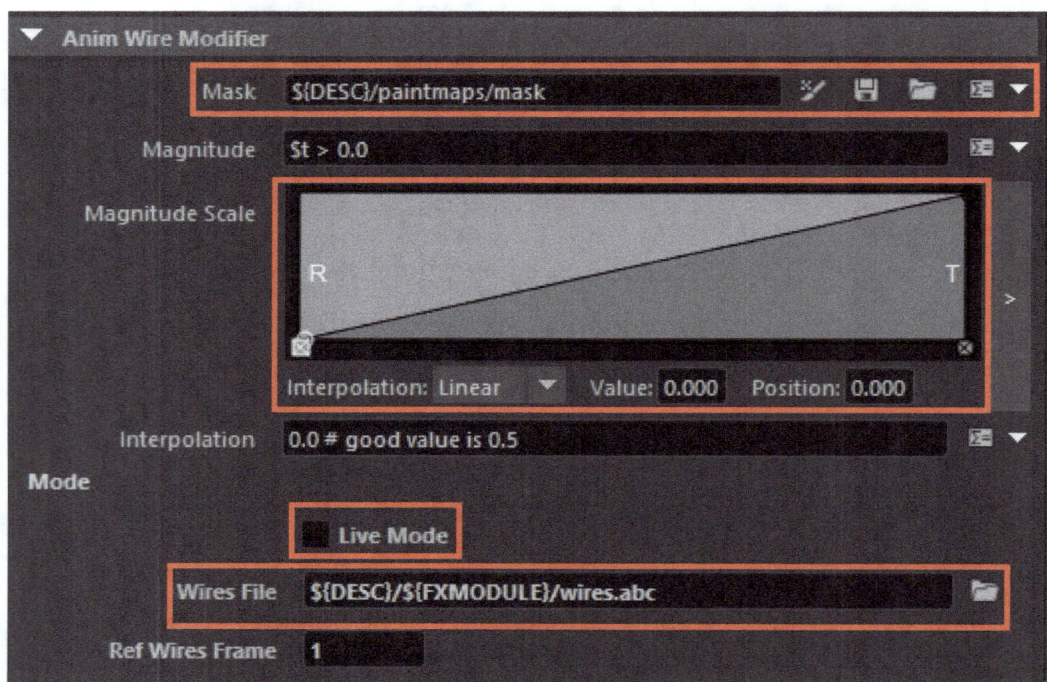

Figure 6.2.2 Applying Alembic Cache To Anim Wire Modifier

Final Caching for Playback and Rendering:

Once the hair simulation is behaving as expected, select all the dynamic output curves and create an Alembic cache just as in the previous method.

Before applying the cache, turn off the **AnimWire Modifier**'s **Live mode** (Figure 6.2.2). Then, apply the Alembic cache and disable the nucleus solver. This will allow Maya to reference the cached data during playback, making the simulation faster and allowing you to navigate the timeline efficiently.

Optimize Performance:

If the simulation becomes slow due to the complexity of the setup, add a **Groom Bake** manager from the **Add new Modifier** menu and move it below **AnimWires** in the modifier stack (Figure 6.2.3). Press **Bake XPD Groom** to cache the modifiers to an external XPD file, reducing the system load and improving simulation performance. Once the XPD file is baked, update XGen to reference it, which will significantly speed up simulation playback.

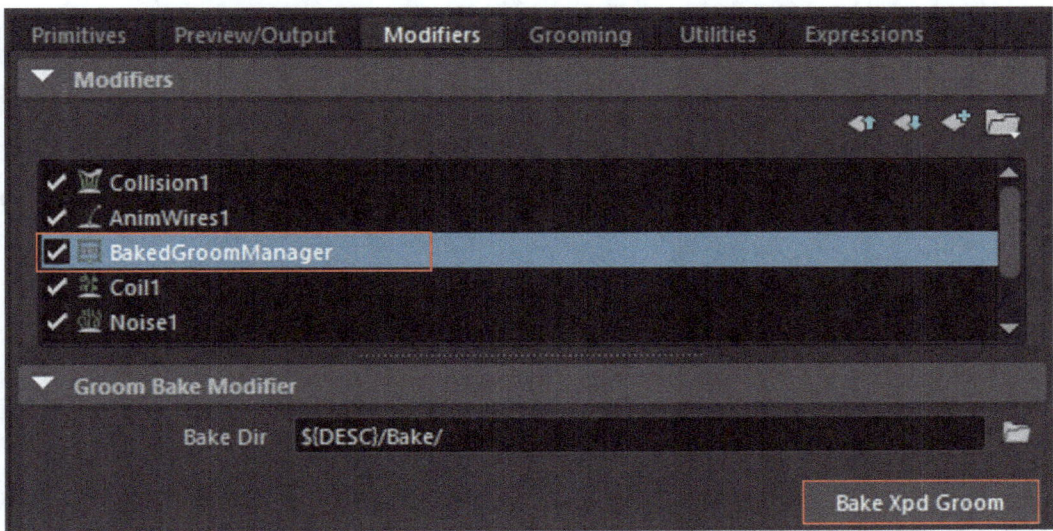

Figure 6.2.3 Groom Bake Manager

Index

A

Alembic Cache: 131, 133-134
    Export Selection: 133
    Apply to Collision Modifier: 133
Anim Wire Modifier: 129, 132, 134
    Creating Dynamic Curves: 129, 132, 134
    Control Map: 132
    Hair System: 129-130, 132-333
Area Lights: 112
Arnold Renderer: 120-121
    Resolution: 2, 8, 18, 21-22, 24, 26, 59, 69, 79, 109, 120-121
    Ray Depth: 121
    Render Settings: 109, 120, 122-128
    Specular: 113-114, 120-122, 124-127

B

Braid Hair: 62, 66-67, 69-73, 75, 104
    Flare Deformer: 65, 74
    Tube Groom: 21, 67, 69, 75
    Wire Deformer: 62-63
Bun: 50, 56, 89-90, 94, 103

C

Clumping Modifier: 31-32, 61, 70, 75, 99-101
    Clumping Map: 32-33, 132
    Clump Scale: 33, 101

Color preview: 100-101
Collision: 131, 133-134
Coil: 36-38, 41-43, 103-108
Curves to Guides: 39, 58, 76, 82
Cut Modifier: 37-38, 103-104

D

Density: 4, 6-7, 17, 32, 70, 79, 88, 90-91, 93-94, 97, 100, 132
Dynamic Properties: 131, 133

E

Expressions: 9-11, 29, 40-42, 116
    Function: 41-43
    Operator: 41
    Variable: 41-43, 122

F

Flyaway: 95-98, 108
Freeze Transformation: 2, 11

G

Guide Control Points: 14
Guide curve: 9, 13-15, 21, 53, 62, 71, 75-77, 81-83, 88-91, 93-94, 97, 130, 132
    Base Curves: 48
    CV: 20-21, 35-36, 48, 51, 56-57, 63, 70, 75, 78-79
Groom Bake Manager: 135
    Bake XPD Groom: 135

H

Hair System: 16, 72, 129-130, 132-133
> Output Curves: 130, 134

HDRI: 110-111,
> Skydome Light: 29, 111, 124

I

Input: 28, 116, 118-119, 121
Interactive Grooming Splines: 6, 8-9
Interpolate: 7, 10, 134

L

Lights: 108, 109, 112
Live: 49, 55-56, 131, 134

M

Mask Map: 59, 69, 84-85, 88-89, 91, 93-94, 96
Modifiers: 8-11, 31-32, 36-38, 54, 61, 70, 75, 88-91, 93-94, 98-101, 104-108, 129, 132-133, 135

N

nCloth: 131, 133
> Passive Collider: 131, 133
> Max Collision Iterations: 131

Noise Modifier: 35-36, 101-103
> Magnitude: 36, 101, 134

O

Output Settings: 23-26

P

Passive Collider: 131, 133
Preview Settings: 23-25, 29-30
Primitives: 7, 9, 10-11, 13-14, 16-24, 31, 35-38, 41-42, 59, 69-71, 79, 81, 84, 129-130, 132-133

R

Reflection: 60, 110, 113, 120, 122, 124-125
Region Control: 21-22, 81
Region Map: 21-23, 81, 86-88, 90-91, 93

S

Scalp Geometry: 3, 45-46, 49, 55, 58-59, 111
> Separate Scalp Geometry: 3

Shaders: 23, 25-26, 30, 109, 113-114
> aiStandard Hair Shader: 113-114
> aiStandardSurface Shader: 28, 109

Simulation: 2, 6, 129, 131-135
> nHair: 6, 72, 129-131, 134
> Hair System: 129-130, 132-133

Skydome Light: 29, 111, 124
Stray: 11, 41-43, 101-103, 105
Substeps: 128, 130

T

Target Guide: 38, 40, 78, 88

Tube Groom: 21, 67, 69, 75

U

UV Mapping: 4, 46

X

XPD: 17, 135

www.ingramcontent.com/pod-product-compliance
Lightning Source LLC
Chambersburg PA
CBHW062106220526

45471CB00010B/3619